THE
GOLFING MIND

THE GOLFING MIND

Vivien Saunders

Illustrated by Ken Lewis

Stanley Paul

London Melbourne Sydney Auckland Johannesburg

Stanley Paul & Co. Ltd

An imprint of the Hutchinson Publishing Group

17–21 Conway Street, London WIP 6JD

Hutchinson Publishing Group (Australia) Pty Ltd
PO Box 496, 16–22 Church Street, Hawthorne,
Melbourne, Victoria 3122

Hutchinson Group (NZ) Ltd
32–34 View Road, PO Box 40–086, Glenfield, Auckland 10

Hutchinson Group (SA) Pty Ltd
PO Box 337, Bergvlei 2012, South Africa

First published 1984
© Vivien Saunders 1984
Illustrations © Ken Lewis 1984

Set in Monophoto Plantin by Servis Filmsetting Ltd,
Manchester

Printed and bound in Great Britain by Anchor Brendon
Ltd, Tiptree, Essex

British Library Cataloguing in Publication Data

Saunders, Vivien
  The golfing mind.
  1. Golf
  I. Title
  796.352   GV965

  ISBN 0 09 155160 9

PHOTOGRAPHIC ACKNOWLEDGEMENTS

For permission to reproduce copyright photographs, the
publishers would like to thank Ken Lewis/Sports Photo-
Graphics and Peter Dazeley Photography.

Contents

Foreword

by Mary Parkinson

A woman's road to golf is strewn with booby-traps. In the main it is the age-old problem of women invading a territory hitherto held by men. In the end she succeeds in spite of the system and not because of it. My golfing ambitions came late and were nearly scuppered at birth, not by traditional male attitudes to women playing any sport, but by my husband's hostility to anyone playing golf.

He formed the 'Anti-Golf Society' some time ago during a holiday in Spain when the travel agent booked us into a hotel along with a battalion of golf enthusiasts. After a week of tripping over golf bags in the foyer and trying to find a conversation that was not about that day's round, he offered a prize to the golfer who had the most miserable holiday. This was handsomely won by a Glaswegian man who never broke a hundred, twisted his ankle in the rough on the last day and then discovered that his wife had been indulging in her own sporting pastime with a local hairdresser.

During that holiday I became intrigued by a game that could command such fanatical devotion from its supporters and such hostility in its opponents. From that day I was hooked.

As I said, the way of women in golf is not an easy one, but my path has been made easier by both knowing Vivien Saunders and reading her thoughts on golf. She has the priceless gift of simplicity. She is able, clearly and intelligently, to translate the complicated theory of golf into language that anyone can understand. This is the teacher's greatest gift and, not surprisingly, she is the National Coach to the English Ladies' Golf Association.

My husband, who disbanded the Anti-Golf Society long ago and now grumbles his way around the course, also holds her in high regard. When I asked him what he thought of Vivien Saunders, he mumbled that if she had been a man and born in Sheffield, she would have been perfect.

She'll know no higher praise than that.

1 This Hellish Game!

The aim of this book is to improve the reader's golfing performance by increasing his awareness of the part the mind plays in the game. The player who has grasped the technique of swinging a golf club and striking the ball reasonably effectively still does not necessarily understand the game. There are many aspects of golf that need to be mastered, or at least discovered and understood, if the player is to make much progress in realizing his true potential.

The player needs to become aware of the limitations of human performance, both physical and mental. He must understand the difference in the mental requirements of performance on the practice ground from those for the golf course; he needs to learn how stress and competition affect him. He must balance dedication and an unerring search for perfection with an inward realization that mistakes and failings are inevitable. The golfer has to be aware of the subtleties of pitting his wits against those of the golf-course architect and greenkeeper. In addition he must understand strategy, stroke play and the head-to-head tactics of match play, while mastering the quirks of his own moods and personality. Finally he needs to combat fear – irrational, destructive fear.

This is not a book about the mechanics of the swing; it is a book about learning, winning, scoring and enjoying the game. It is not a book on physical technique but rather a guiding philosophy for the thinking golfer. The beginner and longer-handicap player are given an insight into the whole learning process, combined with an explanation of the main conceptual problems in the mechanics of the game. The aspiring champion is set on the road to a real understanding of the mental game and hence to optimum performance.

The philosophy of this book is that the golf swing is essentially simple. The game itself, on the other hand, is absurdly difficult to play well. For many players it is absurdly difficult to play at all. This surely is part of the charm of golf, for no one can ever claim to conquer the game completely. Certainly the majority of amateurs find it difficult and frustrating, and many well-coordinated, all-round sportsmen find the game well-nigh impossible. Young children – just to make it worse – make it irritatingly easy. The beginner at golf as a rule finds it a much harder game than any other he has tackled; the world-class player can find it supremely simple one day and can be brought to his knees with a devastating loss of performance the next.

The club player faces three stages in his attempted mastery of the game. Stage 1 is the swing. That, believe it or not, is the simple part. Stage 2 is the skill of shotmaking. Stage 3 is the supreme art of scoring – the most difficult aspect of the game – and, although in part dependent on stage 1 and stage 2, a separate art of its own.

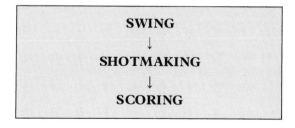

The amateur golfer usually encounters certain difficulties with the swing and shotmaking stages – not because of the complexity of the task but rather through lack of knowledge of a few crucial concepts combined with the inherent problems of adult learning. In many instances he never satisfies his own expectations and aspirations in these stages and almost refuses to acknowledge that there is yet another aspect – the scoring game – to master. To him, golf seems baffling, frustrating, full of unnecessary difficulties. In many ways the game seems all the more frustrating for the player who strives at perfection with the swing and shotmaking, almost achieving it, and yet fails to master the real art of scoring. *His mind may in fact be so intent on technical perfection that he never realizes the scoring art exists.*

Success for the beginner rests on a grasp of the fundamental difficulties and techniques of the game, combined with an understanding of his learning faculties and shortcomings. Success for the club amateur is largely hampered by a few misconceptions about technique, together with inbuilt fears and unproductive thoughts that impede his progress in shotmaking and scoring. His level of success at golf, unlike most sports, is not primarily dependent on physical capabilities. It relies far more on a thorough understanding of the game combined with well-trained mental strengths and abilities. For the top-class golfer and professional, one of the greatest difficulties is in contending with the inevitable fluctuations in the standard of performance which in many ways epitomize the game at that level. In some sports a top player will often become virtually unbeatable throughout one or more sporting seasons. In golf this just doesn't happen. The very nature of the game means that any momentary loss of concentration or confidence can see a champion coming unstuck just as easily as the rank amateur. *For the champion the capacities for concentration and decision-making have to be highly developed to repel any momentary weakness, while the level of confidence has to be finely tuned somewhere between foolish arrogance and a wise humility for accepting inevitable imperfections.*

My explanation of the mental game of golf starts and finishes with a look at fear. Most people's golf games are dominated almost en-

tirely by a fear of failing and by irrational concern over imperfections.

Golf is a game made up of errors. Learning to cope with feelings of failure and imperfections is one of the keys to freeing the mind and allowing oneself to play to the best of one's physical ability. Bad shots at golf can be devastatingly bad; perfect shots are very few and far between. And each shot is critical; it has to be counted and recorded and, to make it even more memorable, it will then determine the next shot facing you. In turn, what happens is that the game becomes dominated by irrational, destructive fear. It isn't the fear of injury or pain as in many sports, but fear of the shattered ego, of failure and embarrassment. It is not the body that requires training to withstand injury but the mind. Free the mind of the fear of failure and the game can be played in an uninhibited, fully productive way. Mastery of the art of playing golf well undoubtedly rests upon mastery of the art of playing poorly. Only by learning to accept imperfection and to play without fear can one perfect both the golf swing and the art of scoring.

The last chapter deals with golf as 'The Game of No Excuses'. In many ways it is necessary to start our explanation of The Golfing Mind by examining our own fears and inhibitions about the game. Most of us are frightened about certain shots, worry about the prospects of a good or bad score and are generally unable to perform in a totally fearless way. Golf is a cruel game and to some extent more terrifying than many others.

Ultimately, success for beginner, club player and tournament professional alike is dependent on an awareness of the game's inherent problems, combined with a perfectly trained golfing mind and sound knowledge of the game's mental challenges and ground rules. The philosophy of The Golfing Mind explores the whole game in terms of its ten fundamental problems. These lie at the heart of all difficulties we encounter, whether as beginner or champion.

Johnny Miller. A moment of lost concentration can be as disastrous – and agonizing – for the champion as for the beginner

The first three – the 'problems of the game' – are the purely physical difficulties of the ball-striking action which unless understood and mastered lead to continual error. From them, as we shall see, stem almost all difficulties with both swing technique and mental technique. The other seven problems – the 'problems for the mind' – form the core of the whole psychology of the game, and can be seen as seven distinct challenges requiring perfect understanding and practice. Without mastery of these seven problems the golfer's skill is incomplete and his game vulnerable to all manner of mental weaknesses. Awareness of the seven problems for the mind produces an inner strength that enables the player to reach new heights in performance.

Developing the golfing mind is therefore initially dependent on an awareness of these seven problems, together with understanding and experience of the mental approach to combating them. Each is complex in nature, throwing out a wealth of challenges and difficulties subordinate to the main problem. The following chapters set out the problems and associated difficulties in detail, leading the reader to an awareness of the techniques necessary to solve and resist them.

This book may introduce you to new rules,

Problems of the game

1   **The perfect strike**
2   **The mystery of spin**
3   **The two-handed game**

Problems for the mind

1   **The overlearning trap**
2   **The invisible target**
3   **The destructive negative**
4   **Trying too hard**
5   **The stationary ball**
6   **Living in the past and future**
7   **The game of no excuses**

---

new challenges and a whole new psychology of the game. It will arouse your curiosity and heighten your awareness of the intricacies of the golfing mind. Through the very nature of the book you will be a more complete golfer by the last page than you are now. As a guiding philosophy it will lead you to internal contentment combined with optimum performance as a golfer.

2 Problems of the Game

The physical, technical difficulties that players encounter with golf usually stem from three inherent characteristics of the game – 'the perfect strike', 'the mystery of spin' and the problems of 'the two-handed game'. Each of these is a separate concept which needs to be grasped in order to combat the usual problems of technique.

The perfect strike

The first of the problems, producing 'the perfect strike', is often at the heart of the difficulties encountered by the novice or average club golfer. It is largely this problem which separates golf from all other ball games and makes it by far the most difficult game for most people to play and enjoy at all quickly. In theory, swinging a golf club should be just as simple as swinging a tennis racket, but for anyone with reasonable coordination tennis is a very straightforward game to start and golf unbelievably difficult. The difference lies almost entirely in the degree of accuracy required in striking the ball. And yet the real difficulty is that the unsuspecting golfer is usually totally unaware of the existence of the problem of the perfect strike.

The teaching professional comes across this lack of realization almost daily. The pupil frequently comes along for a lesson specifically to correct a shank, topped shots or some other impact error. All too often he has two or three practice swings to start a lesson, none of them making contact with the ground in anywhere near the right place, and then will almost glow with pride to the professional: 'There, I can do

it without the ball.' The pupil may be convinced but the professional can see the problem instantly! *The desired accuracy of contact poses just too fine a task for the player and yet, instead of accepting and working on this, his mind is probably burdened with irrelevant technicalities.* As we shall see later, he has now succumbed to the first of the problems for the golfing mind – 'the overlearning trap'.

In golf, the ball is extremely small, sits on the ground – just to add to the problems – and has to be struck by a tiny clubhead. In tennis not only is the ball much larger but the racket head is vast by comparison. For this reason the beginner at tennis can usually make a very adequate contact with the ball at his first attempt and is able to focus most of his attention on where he is trying to hit the ball or, indeed, on the game itself. The movements usually seem relatively uncomplicated and the player can concentrate on getting the ball from A to B.

The beginner at golf can usually produce a reasonable swing without the ball, simply by copying what he sees and with the assistance of a little verbal explanation. Obviously he may need some encouragement to relax or to allow the feet and legs to move freely. But in a comparatively short time – a matter of minutes rather than hours – the complete beginner can usually produce a swing, based on copying his teacher's, which is technically sufficient to make a very good start at the game. So far so good.

The next stage for the adult beginner is crucial. He must be made to realize at this point that his primary goal is to develop the ability to make the clubhead brush the ground at the exact spot where the ball is going to be. This is very obvious and quite logical once you think about it, but the majority of beginners either do not realize or are not taught about the accuracy required. The assumption is often made that a good-looking golf swing automatically produces a good contact with the ball. Of course, it does not. Without considerable skill and concentration, the best-looking golf swing can still come down an inch away from target. Indeed, the beginner's first attempts do not brush the ground just a matter of an inch away from target; he will usually make contact with the ground anywhere within a circle perhaps six

inches in diameter and probably varying in depth by a couple of inches. This, of course, is nowhere near accurate enough to make a good contact with something as small as a golf ball. You are really looking for a contact with the ground at a spot about the size of a small coin. Were both pupil and professional patient enough, the answer would be to keep the pupil swinging repeatedly at this stage, simply aiming at this very strict accuracy before letting him loose with a ball. The accuracy required at impact is considerably higher than most club golfers ever realize or achieve.

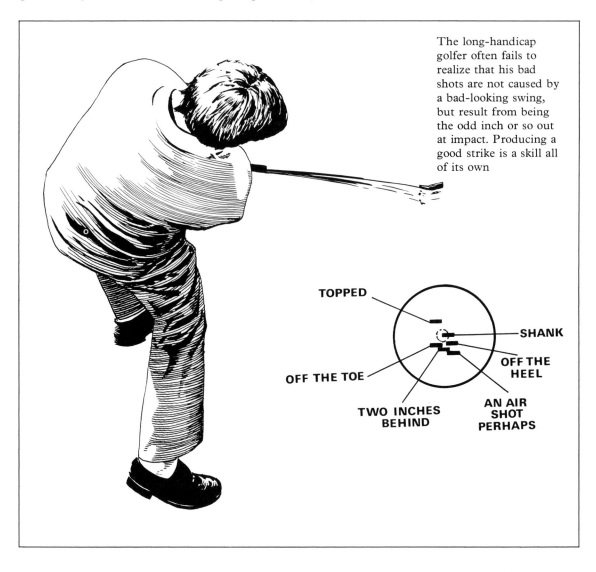

The long-handicap golfer often fails to realize that his bad shots are not caused by a bad-looking swing, but result from being the odd inch or so out at impact. Producing a good strike is a skill all of its own

TOPPED

SHANK

OFF THE TOE

OFF THE HEEL

TWO INCHES BEHIND

AN AIR SHOT PERHAPS

Even the best-looking golf swing can come down fractionally off-target without considerable skill and concentration on the perfect strike

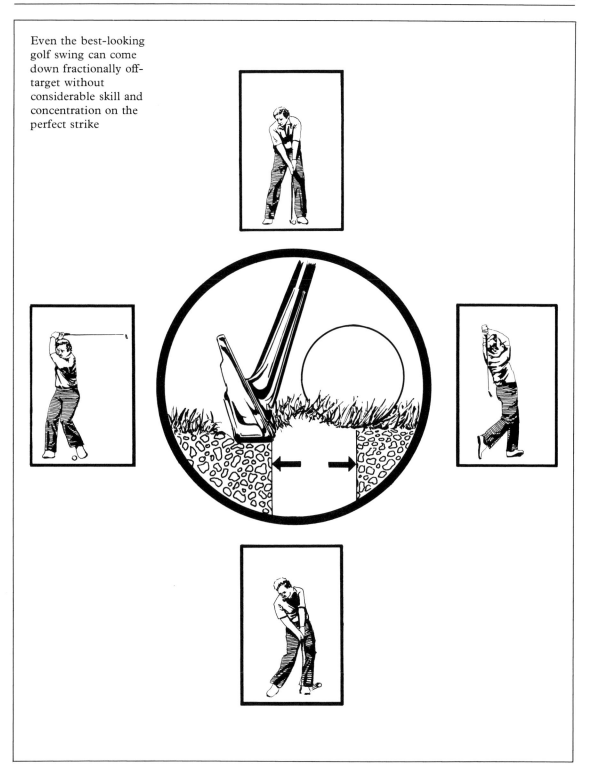

What generally happens to the beginner or long-handicap player is that he starts out by making quite a few presentable swings at the ball. However, he simply fails to make the clubhead come down in the right place. He may come down behind the ball or slightly inside or outside it – in other words, too near or too far from his feet – and the contact with the ball is poor. So what does he do? His immediate reaction is to think he has swung incorrectly. All that has probably happened is that he has been an inch or so out with his judgement. But he doesn't see it that way. Instead of repeatedly practising his swing and trying to make the club come down in the right place, he switches his attention to points of technique which he *ima-*

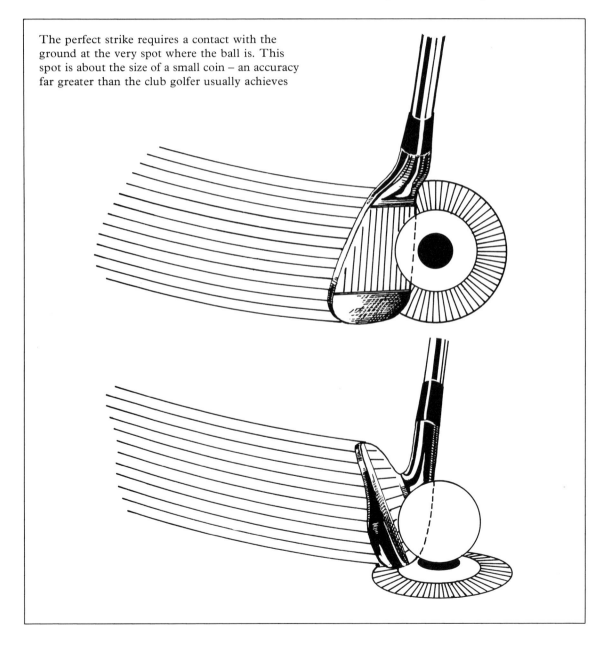

The perfect strike requires a contact with the ground at the very spot where the ball is. This spot is about the size of a small coin – an accuracy far greater than the club golfer usually achieves

gines have some bearing on what went wrong. The swing suddenly becomes difficult. He tries to analyse what went wrong with the swing, instead of concentrating his attention on developing the necessary accuracy of contact with the ground and hence with the ball. If he could only be convinced that he should work for accuracy of contact with his basic swing, all would be well. However, almost all club golfers think of any bad shot as having been caused by a poor swing, rather than realizing that the problem is simply one of bad judgement through lack of experience. *Instead of working on perfecting his contact* before *trying to worry about intricacies of technique, he becomes more and more befuddled by thoughts of his own movements, and the contact is for ever ignored.*

The sceptic who allows himself to become entangled in the theory of the game will at this stage be saying, 'Oh no, a badly struck shot is always caused by a bad swing.' But this is just not the case and can be demonstrated very easily. Next time you are out practising, tee up a ball and address it with your driver. Now take a swing but miss the ball on the inside – in other words, swinging down closer to your feet. This is reasonably simple, and what is important to realize is that you have brought the clubhead down in a different place, *without having to change the idea of the swing*. All that has altered is the idea of your contact with the ground; you have judged it differently. It has not made you think of making any technical change in your swing but is simply a question of judgement. This is at the heart of the majority of really bad shots in golf, and certainly what causes the initial disasters of the beginner is poor judgement from lack of experience. Just as it is possible for the experienced golfer to swing the clubhead through inside the ball, intentionally, without making any swing change, so it is very easy for the novice to bring the club down inside or outside or behind the ball, quite unintentionally, without any noticeable swing change.

This concept is very important for progress in the early stages. Unfortunately most beginners and long-handicap players are not made sufficiently aware of the great accuracy they require. The golfer must be made to appreciate that, whatever he does with his swing and whatever changes he makes, the primary objective of the swing must be to get the clubhead to brush the ground in the right place. Any problem of catching the ball thin or heavy,

The perfect strike – not just the result of a great swing, but of unerring concentration

striking it from toe, socket or heel, comes from a degree of misjudgement and simple lack of accuracy at impact. The error has only to be fractional to cause a less than perfect shot. An excellent discipline is to check the strike periodically by practising with a blob of lipstick or chalk on the back of each ball, monitoring the mark it leaves on the clubface. Correction can be seen to follow from focusing on achieving a perfect strike, rather than an obsession with the body and technique. Even for the low-handicap player and professional, minor errors in the strike are more problems with judgement or concentration on impact than with the technique of the swing. The golfer who can accept this has every chance of building up a simple approach to the game, keeping his swing uncomplicated and striving to perfect his contact and shotmaking.

The perfect strike

Golf is probably unique in requiring a contact accuracy which is far too demanding for all but the skilled player to achieve unerringly. The golfer as a rule fails to realize that the problem of the perfect strike exists. He sees all difficulties as ones of complex technique rather than poor judgement through lack of experience, or loss of concentration.

The mystery of spin

As we shall see, one of the weaknesses of the adult golfing mind is a tendency to reject simplicity and in turn to display an obstinate reluctance to consider the real basics. The second characteristic of the game which is at the heart of the difficulties experienced by the club player is 'the mystery of spin'. *In most games the ball flies in a straight line and the art of the top player is one of putting spin on the ball.* In golf, exactly the opposite is true. The golf ball not only takes up backspin in getting airborne, but

very readily takes up sidespin which takes it curving off line in flight; this is all the more noticeable because of the huge distances involved. Although most golfers are aware that the ball can bend in flight, they generally pay little or no attention to the problems and causes of spin. But this is absolutely crucial to an understanding of the game. The main problem, after all, for almost all but the top-class player is one of eliminating unwanted sidespin and the directional problems that go hand in hand with this. The uninitiated golfer usually makes all his instinctive alterations to technique as though the element of spin did not exist, and in direct opposition to the true correction. Without a grasp of the mystery of spin the game can only be baffling and frustrating.

As we shall see in Chapter 4 there are two distinct elements in the direction of any shot. The first is the direction in which it starts; the second is the way, if any, in which it curves. The two must be treated quite separately. Controlling the initial direction is as a rule fairly straightforward and reasonably instinctive. Controlling the curve in flight, by contrast, requires a sound unravelling of the mystery of spin and the basic mechanics of club and ball. *Unless he has solved the mystery of spin, the golfer's instinctive attempts to correct any curve to his shots are made as though the element of sidespin did not exist.* He sees the shot curve away to the right but corrects it as though the ball had flown straight there, totally ignoring the element of spin. Success eludes him. Even if he is aware of the spin factor, without fully grasping it, he probably subconsciously wishes it didn't exist and so resorts to over-analysis of his own movements rather than looking for real understanding of the whys and wherefores of contact and flight. Yet the preoccupation with intricacy and detail tends to be accompanied by rejection of simplicity and a stubborn lack of interest in the true fundamentals.

Many players find improvement at golf virtually impossible as a result of this complete lack of understanding or curiosity about the mystery of spin. They have no concept of how a faulty flight to the shot is caused by the impact of club and ball. Instead of being able to follow through

Most golfers fail to grasp the mystery of spin. The typical slicer cuts the ball from an open clubface and out-to-in swing, but then tries to correct the shot as though it was pushed straight right and as though the element of spin did not exist. The more he tries to drag the ball left the greater the cutspin he puts on the ball. The mystery of spin eludes him

a logical process of analysing the shot, the strike and in turn the swing, they can only look for improvement through a form of irrational superstition. If the ball doesn't fly correctly, they try this, that and the other and build up superstitions of cause and effect in the swing which are usually totally erroneous – for instance, 'If I tuck my right arm in, I hit a good shot.' Tucking the right arm in probably has no causal relationship with what happens to the shot, but if, by coincidence, tucking the right arm in and a good shot coincide the superstition is built up that one causes the other. In this way players tinker around with their feet and their knees and elbows and head and go on searching for the key that will unlock the door to success.

The club golfer's worst enemies are often his own friends and fellow competitors. They themselves probably understand as little about the golf swing and the mystery of spin as he does and pass on to him all sorts of old wives' tales with a view to assisting him with his game. They will suggest turning his feet in or altering something in the set-up or backswing without any logical reason for such suggestions. This kind of club golfers' technical folklore is produced from nothing more than a superstition: 'I did this and it worked; therefore doing this causes success.' This is really just as illogical as saying that if you happened to be wearing red socks and played well you should therefore always wear red socks for success to follow.

Hubert Green demonstrating the ambidexterity needed for top-class golf, a perfect blending of left side and right side

> ### The mystery of spin
>
> **Rejecting simplicity usually leads to a lack of interest in the basics and in particular the mystery of spin. Without an understanding of spin and of cause and effect in the swing, learning is very much a question of trial and error and theory is nothing more than superstition.**

The two-handed game

The whole philosophy of this book and of my teaching is that the golf swing must be viewed as being essentially simple. The whole action takes only a few seconds and requires the movements to be spontaneous and unforced, thereby giving the mind freedom to concentrate on striking the ball on target. The movements do, however, cause difficulties. As we shall see later, many of these difficulties are self-inflicted and result from falling into 'the overlearning trap'. However, the player who finds the golf swing unnatural usually has problems with coordinating his left and right hand. *Golf is not, of course, the only two-handed game, but it is possibly the only such game where the arms and hands must work in unison through such a large distance.*

For the club golfer, most real difficulties with the physical actions of the swing occur when one side of the body gets in the way of the other,

inhibiting the natural movements. At a more advanced level problems can arise if one side of the body is particularly dominant. Both right and left sides have very important roles to play, and the sport at top level requires a certain degree of ambidexterity. As we shall see in both 'the long game' and 'the finesse game', left and right sides have their specific parts to play, dominant at one moment, subservient the next. Blending the two together with perfect timing and coordination is a necessity to acquiring sound swing technique.

> ### The two-handed game
>
> **A perfect golf swing requires a perfect blending of left and right side, the left side largely controlling the backswing, the right hand generating power at the correct moment. All too easily the right side is over-dominant, the left doing nothing but getting in the way through impact.**

These three characteristics of the game are in many ways quite unique to this particular sport. In no other is the perfect strike so demanding. In other games the mystery of spin requires art and finesse to put spin *on* the ball, not to take it off. Finally, the golfer has to forget his natural right- or left-handedness and learn to coordinate both in harmony if he is to achieve even a modicum of success.

3 The Overlearning Trap

As we saw in Chapter 1, there are several inherent problems for the golfing mind to overcome en route to realizing full potential with the game. The first problem, 'the over-learning trap', in many ways arises from the problem of the perfect strike. Almost all golfers allow the swing to be over-complicated, leaving too little thought for the shotmaking and scoring aspects of the game. In the novice and long-handicap player this is a direct result of the excessive contact accuracy required. Instead of seeing the bad shot as being one of poor contact through lack of experience, he wrongly assumes that it must be caused by complexities in the movements involved. He begins to analyse the action of his body and limbs in an unproductive way, instead of appreciating that the real problem lies in being an odd inch out with the clubhead at impact. He looks for complexities where complexities don't exist.

It is, indeed, well worth comparing the tennis player's approach with that of the golfer. The two tend to be quite different. Yet essentially the tennis player is trying to do something very similar, with movements that are no less complicated. In many ways the movements of the tennis player should be far more difficult than those of the golfer. He has to make constant alterations to allow for the bounce of the oncoming ball and perhaps requires a greater variety of strokes. The beginner at tennis, however, usually allows himself to take a nice, free swing at the ball, uninhibited as the golfer is. The difference very largely stems from the required contact accuracy. *The tennis player makes contact very easily and goes from strength to strength the more he plays. The golfer, by contrast, may find the contact almost impossible, and his performance may even deteriorate as he begins to over-analyse the task.*

Supposing we gave our novice tennis player a tennis racket with the dimensions of a golf club and a ball the size of a golf ball. All of a sudden making contact with the ball would become difficult. He would miss the majority of shots, catch a high proportion off the wood and begin to find the game almost impossible. Yet the actual physical movements involved in playing the game would not change. The forehand drive would still be the same forehand drive and the service action would remain just the same. All that would have altered would be the tolerances for accuracy. One can be almost certain, however, that tennis players faced with this problem would begin to take the same approach to tennis as golfers do to golf. The extra accuracy required in making contact with the ball would probably be ignored but would in turn lead to over-technicality and over-analysis, as in golf.

As we have seen, the accuracy required in golf is so immense – perhaps greater than in any other ball-striking game – that the movements involved are almost always seen to be much more difficult and complex than they really are. At the first sign of any poorly struck shot the golfer will nearly always resort to analysing the movements in his body instead of relying on his swing, working on a perfect strike and eliminating his errors of judgement.

A squad of first-class professional golfers would probably almost all treat the golf swing as relatively simple and natural. If we gradually reduced the size of the ball they were using, there would almost certainly come a point in the

Striking a tennis ball for the good sports player is usually fairly natural, but give the player a racket and ball of comparable size to a golf club and ball and the sport would suddenly become absurdly difficult and the movements, previously thought of as simple, would be over-analysed to the detriment of the player

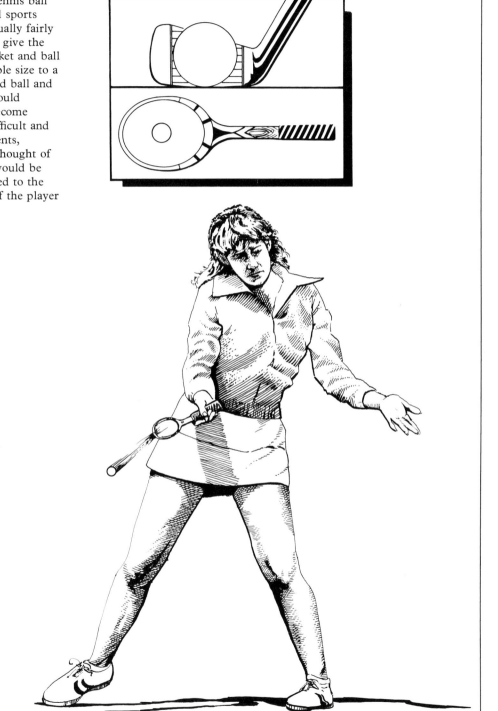

reduction when the accuracy required in striking the ball would become so exact as to produce a breakdown in the physical movements involved. And yet, of course, in reality the physical movement of the striking action would be no more complex. No amount of changing the technique of the swing would make the task any easier. The answer would be to maintain the actions previously used, developing their accuracy even further, but resisting any tendency towards complicating the actions involved. The task would require a heightened awareness of the accuracy tolerances and a different level of concentration and perception. Some of our squad of professionals would almost certainly have sufficient faith in their previously successful technique to try to use the same swing and work purely on contact. Others would possibly become so demoralized by the problem that they would begin to tamper with technique and no doubt eventually lose any natural freedom. They would suddenly be facing the problems the beginner faces.

Conversely, if the beginner were taught with a larger ball and larger clubhead, he would have little problem in making solid contact and would almost certainly begin to treat the swing as the simple action it is.

The good golfer usually sees the swing as being relatively simple. But reduce the size of the golf ball and at some point the task becomes too difficult and technique breaks down. This is the problem the novice faces. The ball is just too small for him to cope with, unless he has an excellent eye for a ball, and this inhibits the development of good technique

> A fundamental need for every golfer is to understand the tremendous contact accuracy required. Instead of working at the perfect strike, he usually sees unnecessary problems with the movements and falls foul of the overlearning trap.

Daring to believe in simplicity

Many readers will by now be wanting to reject this simplistic view of the swing. Some will be rejecting the idea that their fluffed shots or shanks simply result from lack of experience or a less than perfect eye for the contact. Many adults just won't allow themselves to accept simplicity. They want to believe in the mystique of the golf swing rather than accept its underlying simplicity and the possible humiliation of failing with a simple task. *The question you must ask yourself is whether you dare believe in the simplicity of the swing.* Isn't it perhaps rather comforting to believe that the golf swing is complex and that you can so nearly do it? Perhaps just around the corner might be the professional who holds the magic key to success and will divulge the game's untold secrets? Isn't this far more self-comforting than admitting that the golf swing is so simple that young children can do it but you can't? There is, indeed, an understandable reluctance to accept a simplistic view of the swing and the possibility of humiliating failure.

Allowing yourself to learn

Learning to play golf to your full potential, whether to club or championship level, requires a full awareness of your own abilities and limitations as far as skill acquisition is concerned. Most adult pupils at some stage regret not having begun or developed the game as children. In many ways their wishes and regrets are valid. There is indeed little doubt that it is far easier for young children to learn to swing a

golf club well than it is for adults. Ultimately, however, the true mastery of the game by the world-class performer requires a more intellectual approach which only comes with maturity. Adults in many ways are unsuited to learning new physical skills like golf or other sports. Although they have the benefit of years of experience of life these experiences almost work against them when it comes to learning new things. *For the adult pupil of sports it is necessary to have an understanding of the child's successful approach to learning and then to allow himself to adopt this very same approach.*

Golf is a sport that many people learn as adults or even well into middle age. The majority of sporting activities and other physical skills are learned during the years of childhood or adolescence; many golfers, on the other hand, begin to play only when they are well past the ideal learning years. The adult pupil in many ways learns in a completely different manner from the child. To a certain extent, the majority of tasks that adults learn tend to be very strongly linked to other forms of skills: there is usually some transfer of training between one learned skill and another. In this way, the adult is usually simply adapting basic skills and using them in different situations. Many adults can adapt from one task to another fairly quickly by analysing the relationship between the new task and any existing skills, linking the existing units of skills together in a different way and thus adapting to novel requirements relatively easily. The process is one of mental analysis.

In learning to play golf, however, the adult subject is usually faced with a task that seems totally unrelated to anything learnt previously. Instead of looking on these new movements in the way he would have done as a child, he begins to analyse the movements involved to try to relate them to his wealth of previous experience. The adult as a rule finds it difficult to adapt to totally new tasks, and in many instances one can see that the ability to learn which would have been present in childhood has been suppressed or even totally lost. *In voicing his regrets at not learning as a child, what the adult unfortunately does not usually think of doing is to take himself back to his childlike learning process.*

Teaching a child

Teaching a young child to play golf is a relatively straightforward and pleasurable task for most professionals. Teaching an adult, by contrast, is often frustrating and unrewarding. And yet, with some explanation to the adult pupil, the problems need not arise. *The adult needs first to be taught to learn like a child.*

During his formative years, the child is faced with a never-ending stream of new tasks to conquer. He attempts each new action over and over again, frequently failing miserably and yet at the same time being undaunted by or unafraid of such failure. The child's apparent lack of fear of failing means that he simply repeats the actions over and over again and his immense learning ability plays its part without any inhibition. The small child learning to walk is an excellent example of freedom in learning. Although his body is developing physically day by day to cope with the skill more ably, he repeatedly stumbles and falls, picks himself up and tries again. Clearly his thought processes at that age are not highly developed enough for him to analyse what he is trying to do. He makes progress simply through trial and error until his body acquires natural balance and permits him to walk unaided.

In a very similar way, the child of eight or nine years can learn to play golf, or ski, or play most other sports, with far less difficulty than an adult pupil. The difference in the pattern of behaviour between the child and the adult in learning to play golf is very noticeable. The young child will immediately imitate with reasonable ease the movements he sees his teacher perform. The results with the ball are at first almost certainly quite appalling, but the young child simply repeats the movements over and over again without making any real adjustment to his performance. He merely copies what he sees and is quite uninhibited by his initial failure. During these early years when learning ability is heightened, the child seems to be confident that if he repeats something often enough it will begin to work quite effortlessly. After all, at this age, almost everything he has previously attempted results in success. He

probably has not really experienced any lasting form of failure and therefore learns in a totally uninhibited way. His golf swing is developed by learning from watching his teacher and by copying. If he fails at first – which almost certainly he will – he continues with the same actions, knowing that success is almost certainly round the corner. He does not analyse his movements; he does not analyse his successes or failures in a particularly complex way. He is content to imitate and persevere with this imitation until results improve.

The child's approach to anything he sets out to learn shows a simplicity and delightful naïvety which is sadly lost in the adult. The child just *copies* what he sees. He may need gentle words of encouragement occasionally, but as a rule the professional or parents appreciate that all they have to do is to show the child and the child will copy. They realize that the child has certain limitations as far as language is concerned and therefore tend not to conceptualize problems into words. They will simply say to the child, 'Do this', and show the child what is required. The child looks at this pattern and reproduces the movements as accurately as he can. This way of learning is thoroughly natural to the child and, to a certain extent, the younger he is and the simpler his view of novel experiences, the better he will learn. The young child will watch the professional or parent and develop a kind of picture in his mind of the movements involved, slotting himself into this picture so that in his own mind he *becomes* the model he is copying. The child would not be saying to himself, 'Ah yes, he's doing X, Y and Z with his legs or X, Y and Z with his arms.' He would have a vivid picture of the body turning back and turning through with a swish in the middle. This he would copy quite naturally, with virtually no reliance on verbal instructions.

The adult pupil

The adult pupil, on the other hand, has a long experience of successes and failures in other skills which burden his mind. He will tend to have inbuilt ideas of what he can do and what he

A child can look at a visual example, picture the movements in his mind, and copy the movements very simply. The adult, by contrast, usually looks at the example, describes it to himself in words, uses these words as a set of instructions to his body, and produces his own interpretation of the actions

cannot do, and although to some extent he has probably learnt to accept his poor performance at some skills he also has an inbuilt fear of failure which inhibits his learning. His view of life tends to be far more sophisticated, and his thought processes involve greater use of language and less use of pictures and imagination than those of the child. Most children start out with a highly pictorial way of thinking about problems and gradually develop an abstract thinking process with the development of language. In most educational programmes the ultimate object is to develop the child's process of learning to a more adult form of linguistic analysis. In teaching physical skills to adults the process has to be reversed, so that the adult is persuaded to adopt a more childlike, imitative approach to learning and thinking. Those pupils who take to golf most successfully as adults are without doubt those who can persuade themselves to resort to imitation as their basic learning tool and largely to reject too much conceptualization.

The adult pupil frequently looks upon the golf swing in an entirely different way from the child. The teacher probably demonstrates the swing to him several times and the pupil fairly readily copies what he sees. He is then given the ball to hit, whereupon his learning pattern suffers its first breakdown. As we have seen, the contact accuracy required is really too acute for the beginner, requiring an exceptionally good eye for the ball or plenty of practice. The child is usually quite undaunted by the minute tolerances of this striking action and simply repeats the movement over and over again until he produces results. The adult, on the other hand, will perform the swing two or three times in the way in which he was originally shown and immediately finds that his results with the ball are pathetically bad or, at the best, inconsistent. Instead of adopting the childlike approach of blind faith, repetition and lack of inhibition, the adult immediately switches into a process of task-analysis and self-analysis. *If the reaction were 'I know it's very simple but I can't do it', the adult pupil might have the intuition to keep repeating the movement in the hope that results would improve. But, instead of this, he almost always thinks to himself, 'If I can't do it, it must be difficult.'*

At that moment he makes the major mistake of analysing what he is doing. He begins to see a complexity in the skill that doesn't really exist. He loses sight of the fact that what he is trying to do is to brush the little piece of ground on which the ball sits, at exactly the right spot, with the clubhead travelling at speed. Instead, he begins to make too much analysis of the actions he thinks are required. The adult's learning process is so engrained with language that he often finds it virtually impossible to learn by copying a visual example but instead relates whatever he sees into words. He analyses the example he is watching, puts this into words which become his concept of the example, then reinterprets these by giving himself a set of verbal instructions of what to do and what not to do, his brain then interpreting these verbal instructions into the movement it believes is required. Definition is lost at every stage and the pupil's self-instructions are largely misguided. He will then usually put question after question to the professional – about this or that point of theory, about how this or that limb is working – all of which tend to be put into a linguistic explanation that results in an immediate change in the learning process. Mainly for this reason most golf teaching is done through explanation and description, and many professional golfers very rarely handle a golf club during a golf lesson, let alone demonstrate what they require.

Visual versus verbal

One of the great problems in teaching adult pupils is how to steer them away from trying to learn the basic arts of the game through description and explanation rather than through pure imitation. The majority of adult pupils will look at the visual example which the teacher gives them but will almost invariably begin to ask questions about the movements. It is very difficult for the teacher to resist giving verbal instructions and instead concentrate the pupil's attention on the movements he is trying to copy. The pupil often feels he is being fobbed off if he is given an instruction merely to copy the example. He wants far too much information. It is all too easy for the teacher to pander to the desires of the pupil and concentrate almost entirely on verbal instruction and the spoken word at the expense of a simple use of examples. Instead of thinking about the learning and teaching process and thereby moulding the pupil in the way he wishes, the teacher frequently begins to be moulded by the pupil into teaching him in the way he wishes to learn – through an excess of verbal explanation.

The use of language for the learning of physical skills can in many ways be detrimental to success. Even when the teacher takes time to explain to the pupil the relative merits of learning by pure imitation and visualization as opposed to learning from verbal instruction, the pupil frequently shows reluctance to learn through an essentially visual input. To a certain extent the adult pupil not only has to be taught the skill in question but also has to be reminded of or taught afresh the process of learning.

Although I spend much of my time writing about the game of golf, my philosophy in teaching the beginner and longer-handicap player is based very largely on one of example and imitation. I work firmly on the principle of giving the pupil a picture to copy. I try to develop in the pupil the idea of watching my movements and then imagining or feeling these movements with as little language explanation as possible. Although some form of verbal explanation is bound to accompany the demonstration, I try to avoid describing movements as such, but rather use language to focus the pupil's attention on the desired aspect of the movement. In this way the teaching is very much a question of saying, 'No, look, this is what you've done and now, look, this is what you should be doing.' I also actively try to dissuade the pupil from describing the movements and encourage use of a visual input, together with instructions based on feelings and sensations.

Many players who fall into the overlearning trap spend too much time early in their golfing careers *describing* the movement instead of *feeling* movement. There is little doubt that the adult can learn by imitation, but he needs to be rigorously guided into this. Adults undoubtedly imitate far more readily than they imagine. Players frequently talk of an improvement in technique and scoring after watching top-class golf on television. Certainly the coverage is such that this is not due to the commentator's explanation of technique but to simply watching the movements. Some people definitely retain a kind of after-image of televised golf which stays with them many days or even weeks. But what they should perhaps be doing is asking their golf professional to give more demonstration during a golf lesson in order to keep a pictorial set of instructions from which to work.

> **Children learn easily through imitation and repetition. Adults tend to analyse movement instead of imitating movement, seeing problems with the actions which would simply disappear with a little experience and practice.**

Role-playing: an extension of imitation

The child's use of a pictorial example in his learning is often so strong that linguistic input has virtually no part to play. The child frequently extends his use of imitation to the point where he becomes totally immersed in the pictures he copies. The child not only looks at an example and then translates this into a feeling for his own movement, but he actually begins to role-play and 'become' his example. Much of a child's learning takes place through some form of role-playing of this type. Not only do they imagine themselves to be cowboys or Indians, astronauts, or whatever, but children frequently imagine themselves to be specific people. The child may learn many of his skills by trying to perform in a similar way to one or other of his parents and later tends to see himself acting in the same way as his childhood heroes or other admired elders. Much of his childhood play is usually centred round being someone else and being in a different place. His games have a degree of fantasy and imagination, and it is well accepted by parents and teachers that his experience is not confined to his own physical limitations but that his imagination should be allowed to develop fully.

As he develops, the child may imagine that he is playing soccer like Pelé or that he can play tennis like Bjorn Borg. He may imagine himself to be a great scientist or a singer, a film star or a politician. The child's process of imitation is so great that he frequently watches the movement and overall style of his example to such an extent that he 'becomes' the person to all intents and purposes. Thus the child may go out on the tennis court and 'be' Bjorn Borg. He may picture Borg so fully that he actually feels himself to be like the star. He copies the movements, probably subconsciously imitates all the small habits of the player and frequently exudes the type of confidence or behaviour one

can see in the champion. His ability to copy in this way is enormous. If a child copies an adult or a particular hero in this manner it is fully accepted by his parents that this is part of growing up. A child may go out on to a golf course and for those three or four hours almost become Tom Watson or Jack Nicklaus to such an extent that the swing is copied and in time the level of ability gradually grows accordingly. For many older teenagers this form of role-playing may in fact be entirely conscious.

Certainly there are instances in sport where one competitor seems to be so definitely modelled on another that you feel the process can only have been a thoroughly conscious attempt to copy one of the superstars. South Africa's Bobby Cole emerged on the golfing scene as a lookalike and playalike of his idol, Gary Player. More recently, Australian Greg Norman emerged on the golfing scene, not only looking immensely like Jack Nicklaus but also gradually taking on all the Nicklaus mannerisms – and with enormous success. In American college golf one player after another emerges, looking

Most adults can learn far more by imitation than by analysis. Try to imagine yourself in the shoes of your golfing idol. Picture the movements you are trying to copy and slot yourself into these movements with the minimum of verbal instruction

and walking and swinging like Johnny Miller or Ben Crenshaw, until you feel they have all been moulded in the same pattern.

Although this form of learning through role-playing is fully accepted among children, most adults are totally repressed in any form of fantasy or imagination that requires them to 'become' another person. Thus, however much one urged an aspiring golfer to 'become' Jack Nicklaus or Tom Watson or Ben Hogan, it is almost certain that the pupil in question would find this kind of role-playing something of an embarrassment. But in reality this is probably one of the best forms of learning, and certainly the one by which the exceptionally athletic youngster almost always learns his skills. With persuasion it does, in fact, become possible to free the adult pupil from his own inhibitions, and in some cases the adult will begin to appreciate the benefits of some form of role-playing, even though this may not be as extensive and all-embracing as a child's. Many adults believe that role-playing is so alien to their nature that, even if they do adopt this form of

learning through imitation, their public admittance of their fantasies and imagination remains somewhat suppressed and embarrassed!

Adopting a thoroughly childlike approach to learning requires that you actually dare go out on to the driving range or the golf course and allow yourself to imagine you are your golfing idol. Try to cast aside the fears of attempting to perform in the same way, of adopting all the mannerisms and in your mind 'becoming' that person. Picture the actions you are trying to copy and feel yourself adopting the movement. If you can allow yourself to do this you will have a very good chance of developing your technique in the same way. To some extent this is why show-business people do so well at golf. The actor or the mimic is relatively uninhibited in feeling himself to be someone else and will often appreciate the advantages of daring to take on a new role.

If you can persuade yourself to cut out linguistic interpretation of the movements and to adopt imitation and even role-playing as your major learning tools, you have every chance of

returning to a thoroughly receptive childlike learning state.

> **A child's use of imitation is often so extensive that he takes on the role of the person he copies. The adult who will dare to try this may well find his method improving dramatically.**

The overlearning trap

The adult pupil who is not a student of 'the golfing mind' is likely to be hampered in his progress at golf by the first problem – the overlearning trap. As we have seen, both he and the game possess several qualities which tend to steer him towards this trap. He may be totally unaware of the 'perfect strike' problem, may totally reject any ideas of simplicity to counter his inbuilt fears of failure, and may well adopt a linguistic approach to analysis rather than relying on imitation.

The very nature of the game combined with adult learning problems so easily leads to making the swing far too complex. If you can persuade yourself to believe in the *simplicity* of the swing technique, it will enable you to concentrate on the complexity of the shotmaking and scoring aspects of the game. If, on the other hand, you like to look at the swing as being a complex system of intricate movements, then the swing will become difficult and you will have little chance to concentrate on overall performance.

One of the great problems in teaching golf is that many pupils look for far too much complexity in the swing and don't allow the natural movements to take place. Any movement can be broken down excessively and made to appear difficult. If it is broken down in this way, the coordination of the various parts of the body tends to be lost, and so too do fluidity and naturalness. Take any simple movement – using a knife and fork, for example – and examine this in detail. Notice the way in which the hands coordinate, one with the other, the way in which the elbows bend and the way in which the fork is carefully steered towards the mouth, even though the position of the head may change. Without doubt, if you began to analyse all the separate movements involved in this and began to describe each movement, logging the way in which it corresponded with every other move-

Concentrate like Greg Norman on swinging the clubhead on the correct path and to a great extent the natural coordination of the body will produce the right movements. Most adult pupils resist all attempts at a simple approach and search for so much irrelevant information that natural coordination is lost

ment, the whole coordinated system would break down. Try it for yourself and you'll see the problem. *Similarly, analyse yourself walking down a flight of stairs or doing any other fairly straightforward movement and you will see the problems that immediately result from delving too deeply into the actions involved.*

Much the same thing happens with the golf swing. Many golfers begin to look for too much detail right from the beginning of their experience with the game, almost certainly because they are unable to cope with the accuracy of contact. Instead of appreciating that a faulty shot is probably just bad contact through lack of experience, most golfers immediately imagine that the problem must lie in the technique they are using and the overall pattern of the swing. This encourages a tendency to break the swing down into far too many pieces, making the whole thing much too difficult, rather than going to the heart of the matter and developing a good contact.

Beyond the beginner's stage, many club golfers and a large number of professionals tend to have the same problems. Instead of looking at the golf swing as merely a way of moving the clubhead through the correct path, many golfers forget the clubhead and try to analyse every

Any simple movement can be made difficult if you analyse it enough

minute detail of the swing. It is very often difficult for the teacher to resist the pupil's attempts to extract excessive information about the technique involved. The pupil will repeatedly ask 'What do I do with my wrists?', 'How should my right arm move?', and so on, instead of relying on the fact that the body will to a great extent move in sympathy with the

clubhead if the pupil concentrates solely on swinging the club through the right path. Since the body has an inbuilt system of coordination, one movement will usually be correctly offset by another movement; in this way the movements will almost always take the simplest and most efficient form. It is difficult for the professional to ensure that the pupil keeps this simple, uncluttered approach to the game.

If the professional shows any reluctance whatsoever at providing information about the exact movements involved, the pupil usually feels he is being fobbed off when he is told that everything will fall into place if he concentrates on the points the professional puts forward. The pupil is likely to think either that the teacher lacks certain information or even that he is trying to withhold some particular secret about success at the game.

The majority of the world's top teachers rely on a relatively *simple* approach to the swing, leaving time and space for concentrating on the shotmaking and scoring aspects. The better a golf swing, the simpler it generally looks – and, indeed, the simpler it usually is. Tom Watson's swing, for example, appears to be just two coordinated movements, a backswing and a throughswing. Everything moves together, back and then through. Improving and perfecting the golf swing should entail creating simple, efficient movements. Once the basic shape of a golf swing is achieved, one can gradually work at reducing the number of movements to find the simplest possible and most durable swing. The fewer the number of moving parts, the less there is to go wrong.

However, some pupils reject any form of simple approach and crave too much infor-

Tom Watson showing the simplicity of a great golf swing, swinging the club back and through with two perfectly coordinated, efficient movements. The simpler the better

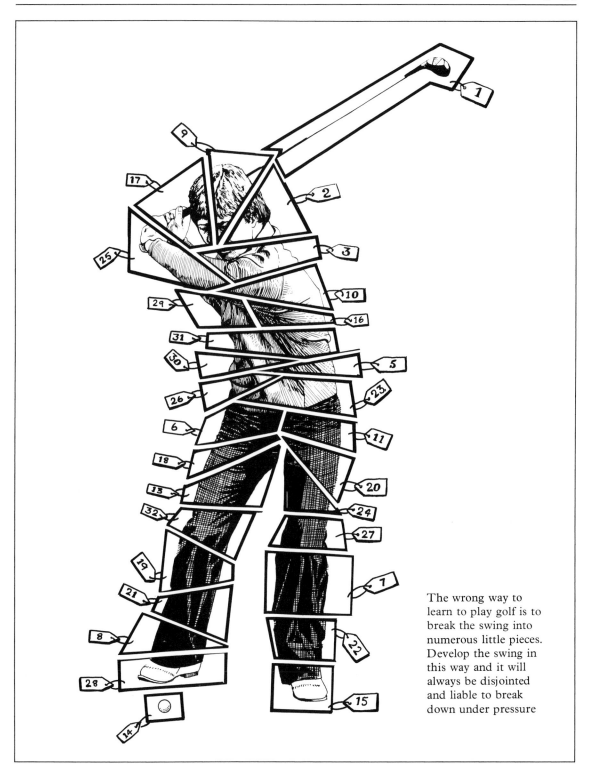

The wrong way to learn to play golf is to break the swing into numerous little pieces. Develop the swing in this way and it will always be disjointed and liable to break down under pressure

mation about the swing and too little about the game. Unfortunately there are some teachers who rely on their ability to make the game over-complicated. Their approach tends to be one of analysing the swing to such an extent that they pride themselves on isolating more minute particles in the swing than anyone else. To a certain type of pupil this excessively theoretical approach to the game has its attractions. The pupil may feel secure in knowing that he has analysed, with the professional's help, every single aspect of the golf swing and the movement of every part of the body at every moment in the swing. The professionals who do teach in this complicated, over-analytical way do nothing whatsoever for the pupil except distort his natural coordination, give him a swing which breaks down repeatedly and usually leaves him so befuddled that performance on the course deteriorates. Sadly this type of approach has been the ruin of many a good young golfer.

Yet who can blame professionals who use this type of ploy in their teaching? After all, many pupils reject all ideas of simplicity and yearn for excessive information and intricacy. If the pro can persuade the pupil that he needs a lesson a week for six months to straighten out his backswing – and that's if he started with a low handicap already – who can blame him? It is a never-ending source of revenue, for the pupil possibly becomes totally dependent on the professional and hooked for life!

> **Many adults are almost afraid of accepting simplicity in case they then fail at something which is acknowledged to be easy. They look for too much complexity and detail from their professional before being ready to cope with it.**

The correct way of dealing with the intricacies of the golf swing should *not* be to build the swing together, piece by piece. *The golf swing is essentially a whole movement and must always be seen as such. The movement takes only a couple of seconds and requires coordination of the*

The correct way of learning the swing is to develop the movement as a whole. From this 'whole', extract points for particular attention, and then

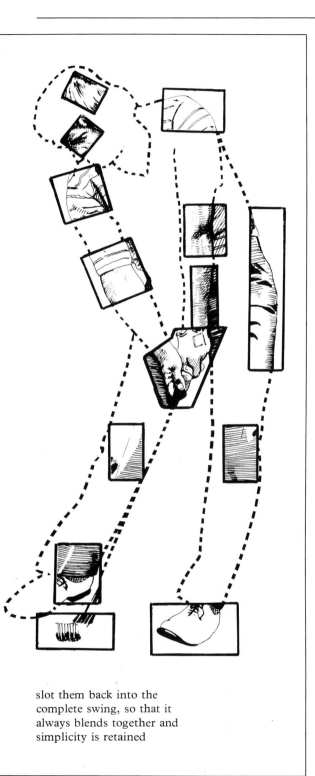

slot them back into the
complete swing, so that it
always blends together and
simplicity is retained

whole body. The first approach must always be to adopt a simplistic idea of the swing as a child would, learning how to perfect contact. This basic swing must be seen as the overall framework into which all other information about the swing is blended. The correct way of teaching the swing is to enable the pupil to see the overall movement and then to isolate any small detail which may require development. Thus if we wanted to focus attention on the top of the backswing we should take this part out of the whole framework, work at it for a fairly brief period of time, and then relate it back to the whole swing before isolating any other part. In this way the pupil retains the overall idea of the swing and makes improvements in relation to it.

Any teaching method which over-fragments the swing is in many ways psychologically very clever and yet from a performance point of view totally disastrous. If the pupil starts by learning the takeaway in his first two or three lessons and then moves on to the second small fragment of the swing, he will immediately get a psychological boost when the professional tells him he has mastered the first stage and is ready for the next piece of information. The pupil is immediately encouraged by his success. He then learns the second stage and is commended when he masters this. He feels tremendous progress when week by week he is given a new piece of the swing to master, little knowing that at the end of the day the tiny pieces can never be blended together satisfactorily and that he will always have a golf swing which is formed of minute disjointed movements. Instead of starting out with a concept of the whole framework involved in the swing, all he has is a picture of a lot of little disjointed units. This type of golfer initially feels that his lessons are a tremendous success because he moves from stage to stage in this way. Although one often sees pupils who are taught like this and treat their teacher as a Svengali who can do no wrong, they ultimately realize the folly of this teaching method and rarely if ever become good and certainly not top-class golfers.

The golfer must be made aware that analysing what happens in the golf swing and learning the golf swing are two entirely different things. To

Try to believe in the simplicity of the golf swing and return to a childlike approach of imitation. Believe the swing is simple and it will become simple, leaving time to concentrate on shotmaking and scoring. Learning a good golf swing is not dependent on analysing every movement involved. Over-analysis of the actions tends to inhibit the body's natural coordination. Remember the magic word 'KISS' – 'Keep It Simple, Stupid'

some extent club golfers have been led into making the swing too complicated by those of us who teach and write about the swing and by the very sophisticated use of high-speed cameras. Either through reading exceptionally detailed analyses of the swing or by looking at a number of high-speed photographs, the player is encouraged to think of the swing as being many small pieces. If he is not careful, he begins to analyse the various positions of every part of the body stage by stage in the swing, without appreciating that the parts of the body naturally coordinate their movements. If one took exactly the same approach towards walking down a flight of stairs, the pupil would find himself tumbling headlong. If he began to look at the way in which the whole foot hinged and moved, the knees bent, the arms swung across the body

or from side to side, and the exact angle of the back, neck and head with every step forward, the natural coordination and balance would disintegrate. Exactly the same happens at golf.

And yet I will repeat that at this stage there will be many a reader who will be arguing against this simplistic approach and attempting to burden his mind with too much complexity. Why indulge yourself in such thoughts? Why not believe in the simplicity of the swing and return to the childlike approach which you know in your heart of hearts is the one to adopt?

The overlearning trap

DON'T assume your problems arise because the swing is complex. Look first at the demands of the perfect strike and master those.

DO dare to believe in simplicity.

DON'T say, if I can't do it, it must be difficult.

DO remember that the swing only takes a couple of seconds and is so easy a young child can do it.

DO remember that children learn by imitation and adopt that as your learning tool. Learn like a child.

DO remember that a good golf swing is simply a way of moving the clubhead through the desired path at speed.

DON'T equate analysis with learning. Analysing everything that takes place in any physical action does not aid learning; it hampers coordination.

DO remember that the swing is only part of the game. Focus your attentions equally on shotmaking and scoring, seeing the complexities in these.

4 The Power Game

Many books are written on the theory of striking a golf ball, setting out to describe the basics and advanced techniques of the swing for the golfer of every standard. It is not proposed in this book to tackle the physical technique of the swing in exceptional detail, since I believe the majority of golfers benefit from adopting a more simplistic view of the golf swing than that with which they usually set out. This section therefore deals with the long game, from start to finish, by examining those aspects that usually produce conceptual problems for the player. Most of the difficulties that players encounter are caused by a failure to understand or totally wrong ideas rather than by physical inability.

The aim of the golf swing

Before dealing with the basic mechanics of the swing, I always like to ask the pupil what he or she is aiming at in the golf swing. Many golfers become so befuddled with theory right from their initiation into the game that they never really think what they are trying to do. Their mind is so intent on keeping a straight left arm, or breaking the wrists in a certain way, that they pay little attention to the ultimate object of the swing. *Remember that the object of every shot in golf is to strike the ball from A to B.* This may seem a ridiculously obvious remark, but many a golfer plays almost every shot without having this objective firmly in his mind.

You should be focusing on several specific thoughts. First, and most important, you should be aiming at swinging the clubhead in a circular path, at speed, so that the bottom of the swing coincides with the bottom of the ball and the direction of the swing travels on target at the moment of impact. To look at the swing in a simplistic way, the body is turned to the right, the arms are lifted and the club shaft is aimed towards the target. From there, the body turns to the left, the clubhead is swished through the ball and the arms lift to the other side. The swing is a turn and a lift, a turn and a lift. What you have to bear in mind is that your whole concept of the swing must be very much oriented towards the clubhead.

Ultimately it doesn't matter what happens to the arms or the legs or the feet or the knees or the shoulders, so long as the clubhead travels on a suitable path at speed through the ball. What golf teachers are really saying when they are looking at an orthodox swing is that the golfers who achieve the best results and swing the clubhead in the best path *tend* also to move their body and limbs a certain way. But this does not mean that one should think that it is *necessary* to move the body in the orthodox way to be successful. Nor does it mean that one should concentrate wholeheartedly on the body and limbs with the assumption that the clubhead will then describe the correct path. This is far from correct. A useful analogy is to imagine yourself throwing a ball underarm. If you want to toss it to the right, you focus on the target and direct the throw there. This in turn causes your arm to swing in a corresponding direction. You don't try to manipulate this; it simply responds to your aim. Just so in golf. In order to develop a good golf swing it is necessary to 'feel' the clubhead so that you can swing it in the chosen path, giving it the necessary freedom to do so by moving the body in sympathy with it.

> **The first key point in the power game is concentration on swinging the clubhead.**

Basic mechanics

In order to make progress at the game, and to learn by understanding rather than struggling with superstition, it is essential to have a full grasp of the mechanics involved in the impact between club and ball. There are four concepts which must stay with you throughout your golfing life as your keys to correcting any faulty

Right: In the good golf swing emphasis is on swinging the clubhead. By this stage in the swing the clubhead has travelled a considerable distance from the top of the backswing. The right shoulder, by contrast, has travelled a relatively short distance, showing no sign of pushing or thrusting to generate power. Correctly the arms and club swing *away* from the right shoulder

The aim of the golf swing is to swing the clubhead in a circular path at speed, the bottom of the swing coinciding with the bottom of the ball, and the swing travelling on target through impact. The swing in its simplistic form is a turn to the right and a lift of the arms, a turn on through and a lift of the arms

shot. The first concept is simplicity itself and, rather like riding a bicycle, once grasped is seldom lost. Simply stated, the bottom of the clubhead should brush the ground and thus meet up with the bottom of the ball in order to get it airborne – the perfect strike. In other words, on standard golf shots, the clubhead should brush the ground at the very spot on which the ball sits in order for the loft of the club to be effective and for the ball to rise. The ball sits on the ground. You therefore cannot strike it on the upswing in the same way as you can strike a tennis ball or any other ball that is hit in mid-air. Any mental idea of trying to lift the ball must be cast out of your mind. If you ever think of lifting a golf ball, ask yourself a simple question: 'How on earth do I propose getting underneath it?' The attack on the ball must be seen as a U-shape or V-shape so that the clubhead swings down into the ball and up again with no attempt to lift it.

Left: The attack on the golf ball must be seen as a U-shape or V-shape so that the clubhead swings down into the ball and up again with no attempt to lift it. If you ever think of lifting the ball ask yourself, 'How do I propose getting underneath it?'

> **If you ever think of lifting the ball, ask yourself: 'How on earth do I propose getting underneath it?'**

The second and third concepts involve the direction of the shot. There are two different aspects to this. The first is the direction in which the ball starts and the second is the direction in which the ball curves. En route to understanding these two concepts it is important to master 'the mystery of spin'. As we have seen, *in most ball games the inexperienced player has difficulty in putting spin on to the ball, and the skill of the champion is usually in being able to make a ball bend to right or left in the air; exactly the reverse is true with golf.* It is very difficult to make a golf ball fly straight and it is only the reasonably skilled player who can make a ball travel without sidespin taking it off line. Your whole instinctive approach to correcting directional faults with a golf ball is almost certain to be incorrect and entirely opposite to the required corrections.

The first aspect of direction is the one in which the ball starts. Assuming the ball is struck from the middle of the clubhead, and not from either toe or heel, it will start in the direction in which the swing is travelling through impact. If a ball starts right of target it means your swing through impact is aimed to the right and if the ball starts left of target it means your swing through impact is aimed to the left. Simply stated once again, this seems logical. However, many golfers who become over-theoretical about the game lose sight of this very important fundamental and will often confuse the initial direction of a shot with the spin that may be produced. Separate the two entirely and always think in terms of any faulty flight as 'Where did it start and how did it spin?'

> **A ball struck by the clubface will always *start* in the direction of the swing through impact. To start the ball on target, the swing must be travelling on target at impact.**

The third concept, also dealing with direction, involves the spin on the ball. As I have already pointed out, the whole essence of playing good golf is to take sidespin *off* the ball and then ultimately to be able to put it back on the ball to produce a curved shot as and when required. A golf ball will fly in a straight line only if the line along the bottom of the clubhead, the leading edge, is aimed in the same direction as the swing at the moment it strikes the ball – in other words, only if the clubface is square to the direction of the swing. If the ball curves away to the right it means that the clubface is open to the direction of the swing, i.e. that the clubface is set away to the right of the direction of the swing. Conversely, a ball will hook or curve away to the left if the line of swing and clubface converge so that the clubface is aimed to the left of the direction of the swing. In order to strike the ball so that it flies in a straight line on target, it is therefore necessary for the direction of the swing to be on target through impact and for the clubface to be aimed in the same direction.

> **There are two aspects to direction: 'Where did it start and how did it spin?'**

The fourth aim of the golf swing is to swing the *clubhead* at speed through impact. Again, the emphasis must be on the clubhead and not on the body and limbs. The force you feel in your body and the strength and power you feel in your arms and legs do not necessarily generate speed in the clubhead. Producing speed in the clubhead is very much like throwing a ball. It is largely an action of the wrists and hands, requiring freedom of movement rather than physical force. Whenever you are searching for distance, return to the concept of *speed* in the *clubhead* as being your aim in the swing. The use of physical force should largely be seen as suppressing freedom and clubhead speed.

> **Distance is produced by clubhead speed, *not* through physical force.**

The grip

In the second chapter we looked at three distinguishing features of the game which in many ways separate it from almost all other sports. There is, perhaps, a fourth problem – 'the game of many weapons'. Golf, unlike almost any other game, involves more than one weapon. Indeed, it can involve fourteen. The player has to achieve familiarity and feel not only for one club but for all. Partly for this reason the player frequently does not develop real control of the clubhead. Each may to a certain extent both look and feel different. But that is not the end of it; golf is perhaps the only game where there is so little contact with the weapon. In the racket sports the player holds the racket virtually continually, learning familiarity with it, developing perfect feel and control. The racket easily becomes an extension of his arm and he begins to know exactly where it is and what it is doing. The golfer, by contrast, takes out each club for its specific shot, picking it out afresh and having to acquire comfort and feel within a matter of seconds. This requires practice.

Clubhead control therefore doesn't come as easily as one might at first assume. The golfer needs to handle a golf club as much as possible, not necessarily swinging it, but at least making friends with it and learning to transmit feeling and sensitivity from the clubhead to the finger-tips. A good grip is therefore vital in developing the necessary clubhead feel and control. The overall concept of the grip, particularly for men, needs to be one of developing sensitivity rather than power. It should be similar in approach to holding a violin bow or an artist's paintbrush rather than a pickaxe or shovel.

Gripping the club correctly also goes a long way towards satisfying the basic requirements in striking the ball correctly. The way in which the club is gripped has a tremendous bearing on the speed that can be obtained in the clubhead and is almost entirely responsible for any side-spin on the ball and the resultant curve in flight. Despite the importance of the grip, it is one of the parts of the game that gives most problems, largely because it receives least attention. Try to face up to the reality that the way in which you grip the club ultimately controls whether you hit the ball straight or not. Indeed, one should never be too proud to go back to the grip at the first sign of a faulty flight. Even the world-class professional can develop minute but niggling errors in the grip, with consequent loss of performance.

In order to grip the club correctly, the hands should feel to be predominantly to the sides of the club, but with the palm of the right hand set

Neil Coles producing clubhead speed and distance through freedom and relaxation, *not* through physical force

towards the target. As the arms swing through impact, the hands return to this position and, with a sound grip, will return the clubface squarely to the ball. In adopting the grip, feel the fingers of the left hand almost pointing along the shaft and then just edge them back and around the club to take hold of it. The tip of the left thumb and first joint of the index finger will then be more or less level with each other. If the fingers are put too much around the club instead of pointing as far as possible along it, the left thumb will be stretched down the club, producing a clumsy position with the wrist virtually immobilized. Once you have taken hold of the club in the correct way, the left hand should be eased into a position slightly on top of the club so that the line you can see between your thumb and index finger points up to about the right ear or right shoulder.

In setting the right hand on the club, whether you adopt the Vardon grip or the interlocking grip, the fingers of the right hand should also be set very much along the shaft of the club and then wrapped around it so that once again the fingers and hands give the impression to anyone looking at the grip of being long and fairly elegant. If, instead, you push the fingers straight round the shaft and take hold of it, the grip will look clumsy and the thumb will stretch too far down. As the right hand is folded over, the left thumb should sit snugly into the palm of the right hand with the right thumb just fitting to the left side of the centre of the grip. The right thumb should not, as many players wrongly believe, point straight down the front of the grip. Again as you look down at your own grip, you should see a line, or this time a V, between the thumb and index finger, which should follow the pattern set by the left hand and thus point up to the right ear or right shoulder. In this way the right hand will be predominantly behind the shaft of the club and therefore set to produce maximum speed in the clubhead, aimed at the target.

The exact positioning of the two lines between the thumb and index finger is really the key to cutting out unwanted sidespin in the flight of the ball. If the 'V's are moved outside the right shoulder – that is, with the left hand

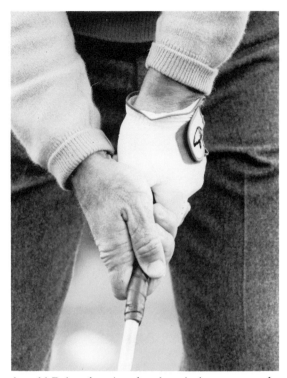

Arnold Palmer's grip – hands pointing very much along the shaft of the club, right palm behind the club, Vs in both hands pointing up towards the right ear, right thumb and index finger on either side of the club

very much on top of the grip and the right hand very much below it – there will in theory be a tendency for the hands to return the clubface into a closed position so that the ball hooks away to the left. In practice, the experienced player who tends to adopt this grip may subconsciously fear a hook and shy away from it during impact by blocking his hands from moving freely and in consequence push the ball to the right. With this grip, however, the underlying fault of a hook always tends to be there. Conversely, if the lines are allowed to point up to the chin or even left of it there will be a tendency to return the clubface in an open position which allows the ball to slice away to the right. Fiddling around very slightly with the exact positioning of the hands will eradicate most problems of consistently hooking and some of the problems of the habitual slicer.

The good golf grip is maintained perfectly from the start of the swing to the end. Here we see the overlapping of the right little finger and the gap between right index finger and second finger, producing a 'triggering' effect for added power

a degree of tension in the left hand but this is only in order to bring it up to the strength of the right.

However, what you must bear in mind is that speed in the clubhead is very largely dependent on freedom and relaxation in the wrists. This is particularly important with driving and the other full shots of 'the power game'. To this end, most players must ensure that the wrists remain relaxed throughout the swing, even though the hands obviously need to retain a reasonably firm grip on the club. Many women golfers in particular need to feel a certain firmness in the hands in order to avoid a tendency to let go of the club throughout the swing. However, for the trained athlete and physically strong individual who takes to golf, it is often necessary for the grip to feel uncomfortably loose and relaxed and slightly out of control in order to obtain the necessary relaxation in the wrists. It is usually only the player of a very high standard who ever has to work at extra firmness in the grip, but for him the problem shots are almost entirely opposite to those of the club golfer. The key to maximum clubhead speed is to maintain the correct combination of firmness and strength in the fingers together with looseness and relaxation in the wrists.

> **The power in the right hand should be *behind*, not beneath, the club; lines between thumbs and index fingers should point to the right ear or shoulder.**

> **Don't look for a feeling of power in the grip. Search for elegance, sensitivity and freedom to enable you to develop maximum clubhead speed.**

With the hands in this position it is essential to adopt the right combination of tension and relaxation in the hands. For the majority of right-handed golfers, it is often necessary to concentrate on firmness in the left hand so that the left and right hands do virtually the same amount of work in the golf swing – the first facet of the problem of 'the two-handed game'. It is not a question of slackening the right hand to enable the two to be symmetrical, but far more one of concentrating on firmness and possibly

The good player *should* be able to adopt his golf grip easily. The left hand should be placed on the club, the right hand added, producing an instantly comfortable grip. Most of the world's great players do this. All too often players show discomfort at setting their hands, adjusting them several times, re-gripping and frequently showing nervous mannerisms which worsen under pressure. It is essential for any aspiring tournament player to be able to set the left hand on the club in one movement, follow it with the right hand and be instantly ready for action without the merest sign of fidgeting. Only in this way are the hands likely to remain absolutely constant throughout each round and each golfing season. It is all too easy to adopt a grip and then allow it to alter just prior to or during the takeaway. The player must check the grip for consistency, fighting any fidgeting, and occasionally returning the club to address from the end of the swing to ensure there has been no movement. Inconsistency of this kind again stems from the lack of continuity in holding the club during the game, since the club is always pulled out afresh. It needs a systematic approach, with a golfing friend or mentor monitoring your twitches or fidgets to eliminate them even under pressure.

The set-up

The set-up, like the grip, is one of the most neglected parts of the golf swing, although its importance cannot be stressed too firmly. The set-up does a number of things that are crucial to playing good golf. Unfortunately it is not a part of the game you can ever ignore safely with the assumption that, once you have learnt it, faults are not likely to recur. *For the good golfer any problem with the golf swing nearly always stems from some alteration in the set-up.* Even a displacement of an inch or so in the feet or shoulders may cause severe problems in the swing. For most golfers, even of top class, the set-up is constantly varying from day to day and needs to be monitored carefully.

There are three main aspects of the set-up. The first is the preparation for the swing, the second the way in which the swing is aimed, and the third the way in which the position of the ball determines the contact and direction of the shot.

SET-UP =	**PREPARE**
	POINT
	POSITION

Ben Crenshaw preparing for the swing, arms hanging relaxed, right shoulder and elbow naturally dropped below the left, left foot turned out a little, knees knocked in

Preparation

As far as the first aspect is concerned, the set-up should be aimed at preparing the muscles in the body to produce the swing. When you are addressing the ball, the weight should be slightly on the insides of the feet, with the left foot perhaps turned out slightly more than the right, the knees slightly flexed and if anything knocked in fractionally. Even though the legs may be flexed very slightly, the hips should not be allowed to drop. Instead the feeling should be one of standing up tall as though someone

Crenshaw stands tall to the ball at address, giving the left leg space to work correctly through impact, producing firmness and stability

were pulling you up from the back pockets. In this way there is room for the legs to move and for the left leg to become firm through impact to provide stability in the swing. One of the real keys to a good golf swing is a perfect, constant balance. A high-hip position is essential, giving the necessary space for the left leg. A low-hip position produces crumpling legs or a bobbing up and down movement. With the knees knocked in the legs are encouraged to move correctly, with the left knee pointing in behind the ball as weight is transferred on to the *ball* of the left foot in the backswing – *not* with a rolling on

to the inside – and enabling the right foot to spin through on to the toes as the throughswing takes place.

As far as the arms are concerned, the left arm should provide the necessary width for the backswing, feeling able to initiate and be in control throughout the backswing and the start of the downswing. For this reason, at address, the left arm should *hang* virtually straight, not stiff, while the right arm is relaxed and tucked in very slightly, setting it up for the position it will adopt at the top of the backswing. One can see here a slight problem in that the right hand is below the left on the grip and yet the left arm is the one to be kept straight and the right arm is to be relaxed – again a difficulty of the two-handed game. This means that the right shoulder has to do one of two things. It will either drop several inches below the left or be pulled forward several inches. Care must always be taken to ensure that the right shoulder *drops* and never pushes forward, or alignment and direction will suffer.

Another point of preparation for the swing is the positioning of the feet. If the right foot is turned out very slightly, this will produce freedom to turn fully in the backswing but is likely to inhibit the turn through of the throughswing. Conversely, if the left foot is turned out at address, this may inhibit the turn of the backswing but will allow plenty of freedom in the throughswing. The generally accepted positioning of the feet is for the left foot to be turned out very slightly and for the right foot to be pointed virtually straight ahead of the player. However, any difficulty in turning back or through in the swing can often be dealt with fairly simply by turning either foot out slightly to encourage rather more freedom in the required direction. Do remember, however, that freedom in one direction is likely to mean inhibition in the other direction. An alteration of even a few degrees can change the feeling of the swing quite considerably.

Aiming

The second aspect of the set-up is to aim the whole swing on target. The main problem here is that most people find it psychologically difficult to aim correctly when standing sideways to the target in the address position. In correctly adopting a 'square' stance, the line across the feet, knees, hips and shoulders should be parallel to the line of the proposed shot. The player is, as it were, standing along a pair of railway lines with the ball setting off down the right-hand one to the target and the body lined up along the left-hand one. For many golfers setting up in this way is far from natural. The most common error is to line up with the feet aimed right of target.

Much of the problem arises from a visual distortion at address. You are, after all, trying to judge a straight line from the ball to the target with two distinct handicaps. First, the player has to judge this straight line without having the eyes directly over this line. This leads to the first distortion. Second, the player has to judge this straight line by standing sideways to the target

rather than with the benefit of looking straight along the line. These two factors lead to varying amounts of distortion, presumably depending upon the individual's eyesight. But, for many, seeing this straight line from the ball to the target and then setting up parallel to it is by no means easy and, for some, wellnigh impossible. Anyone who suffers from this type of visual distortion will almost always find problems with lining up. Unfortunately the player who lines up incorrectly almost always begins to compensate for the error and this in turn leads to problems with the swing direction.

The best way to overcome this type of distortion and error in alignment is to develop a routine for lining up whereby the straight line can be judged from behind the ball–target line. For the person whose natural aiming is less than perfect, the correct way to line up is to stand directly behind the ball–target line and to choose a spot on the ground 15–30 inches ahead

Right: Larry Nelson at address, standing tall, hips up and out, with lines across feet, knees, hips and shoulders all parallel

Below: Jack Nicklaus taking a few moments on the practice ground to check alignment

of the ball; the player can then concentrate on lining up over this spot rather than trying to use the target in the distance. Having chosen the aiming spot, the player should then take up the address position, setting the clubhead and then the feet and shoulders parallel to this imaginary line on the ground. In this way the player has something far clearer to line up with than a distant target, and the likelihood of visual distortion causing errors is reduced. Some golfers prefer to keep this spot in mind throughout the whole shot, without ever looking up at the target again until the end of the swing, but relying on a mentally retained image of the target. Other players like to get themselves into position relative to the spot but then look on up at the target a couple of times before executing the shot. The danger, of course, in doing this is that as you look up at the target you are likely to feel misaligned and may therefore shift your feet around into what feels a comfortable position.

tion. For anyone who does suffer from a visual distortion in alignment there are real merits in adopting a definite ritual in setting up – choosing the spot on the ground, lining up over this and then really trusting yourself to have chosen the right spot so that you concentrate on hitting the ball out over it.

> **To avoid aiming distortion, choose a spot on the ground to aim over; have unerring self-belief in your choice and focus your attention on starting every ball out over the spot.**

Almost more important than the line of the feet, however, is the line of the shoulders. The line of the shoulders will really determine the direction in which the clubhead travels through impact. In dealing with the first aspect of the set-up, the preparation for the swing, I mentioned that the right shoulder has a tendency to come forward at address, rather than dropping below the left shoulder as it should. This often means that the turn in the backswing is insufficient, so that the shaft of the club usually points away to the left of the target instead of pointing on target at the top of the backswing. Keeping the right shoulder back in the correct position so that the line of the shoulders aims on target is often a fundamental problem. This is partly because the right hand is below the left and thus pulls the right shoulder ahead of the left. Problems also arise because the player tends to be thinking about the target and therefore often turns the upper body towards the target in taking a last look down the fairway before striking the ball. Care must always be taken to set not only the feet but also the shoulders square to the line of the proposed shot.

Bernhard Langer showing the classic set-up position, right arm tucked in a little to keep the right shoulder down and back, parallel to the target line, rather than allowing it to be pulled forward

Ball position

The third factor in the address is the position of the ball in relation to the left foot or the right foot. This is perhaps a part of the game which causes most confusion for the club golfer, largely because teaching professionals often feel that the club golfer should adopt a different ball position from that used by the tournament professional. Tournament professionals will frequently say that they play all their shots from opposite the left heel, whereas teaching professionals will often suggest that the player play most shots more centrally in the stance, or alternatively adopt a graduated ball position, with the long irons played opposite the left foot and the shorter irons played more towards the centre of the stance. In their own way, of course, each of these theories is correct. What should be appreciated is that, since the tournament professional generally uses much more hand and leg action, the bottom of his swing is likely to fall nearer to his left foot than does that of the average golfer. The older golfer and most women golfers, in particular, will usually find that the natural bottom of their swing tends to fall more or less opposite the centre of the stance, so that it is around this point that all alterations should be made.

In adopting a ball position, then, the first requirement should be to determine where the bottom of your own swing naturally falls. For the professional golfer this will usually be more or less opposite the left heel, but for most golfers the bottom of the swing will naturally fall perhaps a third of the way from left foot to right foot. This should be the basic position from which most standard golf shots are played, with the clubhead striking the ball at the natural bottom of the swing. If the ball is positioned slightly to the left of this – i.e. further forward in the stance – there is a tendency to catch the ball very slightly on the upswing; conversely, if the ball is played slightly further towards the right foot, there is a tendency to catch the ball slightly on the downswing. By using this very logical piece of information you can see how the ball position can be varied according to the lie of the ball. If the ball is lying on a nice cushion of grass, it can be contacted slightly *beyond* the bottom of the swing so that the clubhead is almost catching the ball on the beginning of the upswing. The ball can therefore be played a little bit nearer the left foot, and this will encourage maximum speed as well as helping to produce maximum carry to the shot. On the other hand, if the ball is sitting in a slight depression or is on a downhill lie, the ball should be struck with the clubhead travelling slightly on the downswing. This will help to squeeze the ball out of the ground and produce a clean contact, striking the ball and then the ground beyond it. For this reason the ball should then be played slightly further back in the stance, so that it is a little bit nearer the right foot.

By using this theory we can see why there is a graduated ball position for the various shots. With the driver the ball should be teed up perhaps an inch or so off the ground so that the ball can be caught slightly on the *upswing*. This means that the ball can be played opposite the left foot and struck beyond the bottom of the swing. The bottom of the swing will still fall in roughly the same place but the ball is caught some six or eight inches later than for a standard-iron shot. On the other hand, with the wedges and the other short irons and recovery shots, the ball should be struck with a *downward* blow, so that the ball is positioned slightly further back in the stance.

Determine the natural 'bottom' of your swing. A downward attack requires the ball to be played further back. An upward, sweeping contact needs the ball to be further forward.

One other piece of logical thinking about the ball position can help to explain many of the problems of direction which creep into most golfers' games. Not only should the ball be caught with the right contact, but it is obviously essential that the swing should be travelling in the right direction at the moment the ball is

The further back the ball is played the more of a downward attack is encouraged – for the short irons, or a bad or downhill lie. But in turn the ball is then often caught before the club is travelling on-target and the tendency is to start it right of target

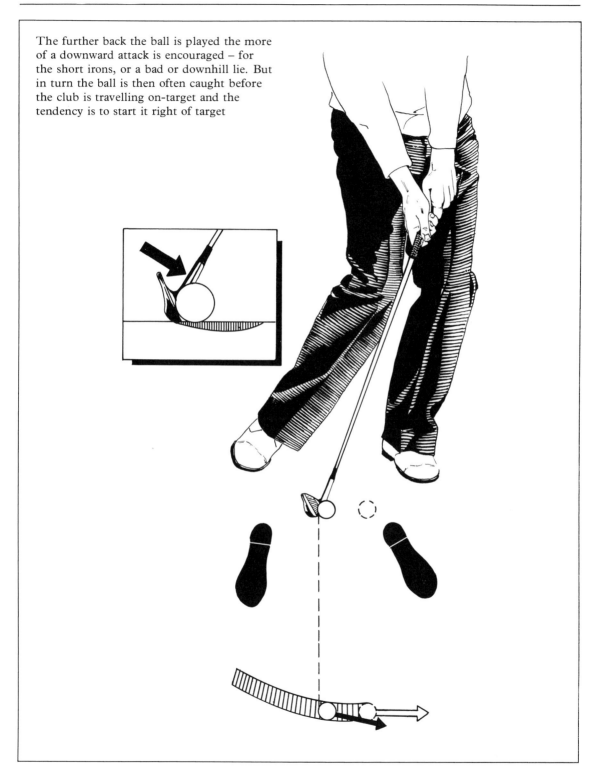

struck. If the ball is played slightly further back in the stance, i.e. towards the right foot, the ball is being caught a little bit earlier in the swing. With a reasonably orthodox swing the clubhead is now not usually travelling on target as the ball is struck, but the line of the swing tends rather to be aimed slightly right of target. For this reason, the majority of golfers will find that when the ball is played further back in the feet the tendency is to push the ball slightly right of target. On the other hand, when the ball is played further forward in the stance with the driver or with the long iron from a nice, grassy lie, there is a tendency to catch the ball beyond the straight-through part of the swing so that the ball will often start to the left of target. In each of these cases it is therefore often necessary to make an alteration to the direction of the stance so that the ball will still be started on target.

> **With the ball back in the stance the attack tends to be right-aimed; with the ball forward in the stance the attack tends to be left-aimed.**

Setting up for consistency

Maintaining a constant ball position, particularly with the driver, is often at the heart of consistency for the good golfer. It is equally important to adopt the correct distance from the ball and not err from this. Good golfers usually stand far closer to the ball than feels comfortable for the club player, keeping the hips up and back, the hands more or less directly beneath the chin. This enables the club to be held on its target line well through impact and encourages perfect balance. Providing the hips are kept up and back, it is virtually true to say that the closer you can stand to the ball the better. Obviously there are exceptions, and the long-handicap player or novice may interpret this to give himself insufficient space, but for the single-figure-handicap golfer it is certainly a good rule of thumb. Distance from the ball

tends to vary from time to time, and a couple of inches' difference soon leads to loss of form and erratic direction. All too easily in the middle of the purple patch one can get over-confident, particularly with the longer clubs, and gradually creep further and further from the ball, producing a slide back to mediocrity.

Similarly the sideways positioning of the feet in relation to the ball can easily alter – fractionally too far forward producing a pull or sway, slightly too far back leading perhaps to a push. Don't be fooled into thinking it will stay consistent; it won't. You can to a certain extent gauge the distance from or position of the ball by laying a club down on the ground as a guideline – remembering which club you have used for future comparison. However, for the serious tournament player a better way is to record the set-up position during a good golfing spell, standing on a sheet of newspaper, for example, and marking the feet and the ball positions and the club used. This can then be referred to at a later date if performance deteriorates, often showing quite a noticeable change.

A further piece of golfing wisdom about the set-up is to check the position of the ball in relation to the clubface. There is something of an optical illusion to this. Set up to the ball with it seemingly opposite the centre of the clubface. Now hold the club steady and view it directly from above or behind the ball. The ball is usually far closer to the heel of the club than the player imagines and may cause added difficulty in contacting the ball from the sweet spot.

Backswing or throughswing

Many golfers are accustomed to think that the backswing is the all-important part of the golf swing. Frequently the golfer is under the impression that if he performs the backswing perfectly the rest of the swing must necessarily follow. To my mind, however, this is the wrong approach to the golf swing, and is often the result of being made to concentrate heavily in early lessons on the backswing with very little emphasis on the throughswing. The player may then stop having lessons before the professional has time to teach the throughswing as fully as he would like. Alternatively the professional may be backswing-oriented. The backswing also tends to be emphasized because by the nature of the game professionals teach the player from behind the line of the shot and can therefore very readily see what is wrong with the backswing; faults in the throughswing are considerably more difficult to pinpoint and analyse. If professionals were able to teach from the safety of a net directly on the pupil's target line I am sure they would give greater emphasis to teaching the throughswing. This would encourage the pupil to give weight to what in reality is the more important part of the action.

A further comparison with tennis is a useful one. Almost all concentration for the club tennis player – and here I am not talking about the tournament professional – tends to be on the forward movement. Emphasis is on the throughswing and the rest just happens. The approach remains simple, and for this reason you don't hear tennis players coming off the court lamenting over problems of 'not being able to take the racket back today'! In golf, by contrast, many a player suffers from a virtually paralysing obsession with the backswing. The brain is thus unable to concentrate on the throughswing and target.

To repeat our most basic concept of the golf swing, the whole idea is to hit the ball from A to B. The most important part of the golf swing is therefore the part in the impact zone. The rest of the golf swing is purely and simply aimed at producing perfection as you strike the ball. *Certainly the backswing goes a long way towards setting you up for the downswing, but what you must realize is that the downswing and throughswing are the crux of the swing and determine whether or not the ball is hit correctly.*

Many golfers believe that if they get to the top of the backswing successfully the downswing and throughswing will automatically follow. This is just not the case. If you look at almost any golfer you will see that his or her backswing repeats itself over and over again with very little variation. Certainly if you look at the professional golfer you can see that the club slots itself

into exactly the same position on virtually every swing. Why, then, does one get a variation in the shots produced? The answer is that, however good and consistent the backswing, the downswing and throughswing are liable to some sort of variation. In order to produce a perfect, repeating golf swing, you must concentrate on both ends of the swing. If anything, I would suggest that the throughswing and end of the swing are more important.

If you concentrate very largely on producing a firm, repetitive throughswing, you will almost always find that the backswing falls into place

Gary Player at the moment of impact. The whole golf swing is aimed at producing perfection at this moment, the backswing simply being preparatory for the down and throughswing

quite easily and the problems you may previously have had with the backswing gradually iron themselves out. Many golfers spend hour upon hour at the driving range or on the practice ground learning to groove a backswing. You see them swinging over and over again without bothering to swing on through and complete the swing. And yet how often do you see a golfer practising the throughswing and trying to develop a firm followthrough? Very often golfers will say: 'Ah, yes, but what can learning a followthrough do? It all happens after the ball has gone and therefore cannot affect the flight of the ball.'

The Nicklaus followthrough, always identical. Aiming at swinging the club through to a perfectly balanced, repetitive finish produces consistency through impact

What you have to appreciate is that, in concentrating very largely on the way in which you swing the club through and in working on producing a definite position at the end of the swing, you are setting the club on the right path to swinging itself through impact correctly. In other words, if you swing the club from the top of the backswing through to a certain position in the followthrough, the clubhead must pass along a certain path through impact. If you concentrate on swinging the clubhead from a perfect backswing position into a perfect followthrough position the clubhead will be correctly or virtually correctly 'positioned' through impact. If, on the other hand, you concentrate only on swinging from the top of the backswing to the ball and imagine that everything beyond impact is of no consequence, it is all too easy to allow the clubhead to come off the correct path and to produce a ragged, unbalanced followthrough which usually reflects poor contact with the ball.

The backswing

The backswing should therefore be treated *not* as the crux of the whole swing but as an action that is preparatory to the most important part of the swing – that of making the clubhead travel correctly through impact. *As far as the backswing is concerned, this should feel to be a turn of the left side of the body combined with a lifting of the arms.* It is important to stress a turning of the *left* side of the body. If you concentrate on turning the left side, the shoulders will be nicely rounded inwards at the top of the backswing. If you think of turning away with the right side of the body the shoulders will be stretched apart so that the chest incorrectly expands. Again it is important to stress that golf is a two-handed game, with the left hand entirely dominant in the backswing. Turn the left side of the body, bringing the weight forward from the heel of the left foot on to the ball of the foot. There should be no undue dipping of the left shoulder. Instead the left shoulder should simply come round as the body turns, slightly covering the chin. Having initiated the backswing with this turning of the body and with the left arm swinging across the chest, the arms – stressing in particular the left one – are then lifted so that they move freely and independently of the body. *At the top of the backswing the plane of the arms should be higher than the plane of the shoulders.*

The hands and wrists should feel active right from the takeaway, with the wrists naturally hinging into a position where the left thumb supports the club at the top of the backswing. The left wrist should be very slightly cupped, with the shaft of the club pointing on target and the line along the leading edge of the club following the plane of the left arm. For the club golfer the backswing should simply feel to be a turn of the body combined with a lifting of the arms, the left thumb positioned in a supporting role. The backswing should become more technical than this only when the player is of a medium- or low-handicap standard. At this stage he may be striving for an accuracy in his game that would warrant fiddling around with the odd half-inch here or there in his exact positioning. Aiming at too much exactness in

the backswing before it is really justified usually leads to unnecessary confusion and inhibition. So the backswing should be kept simple and treated as preparatory to the throughswing.

> **The backswing should be left-side dominated. Keep it simple and treat it as purely preparatory to the throughswing.**

When the player reaches a more advanced stage and has developed the overall shape and rhythm of the golf swing, combined with purity of contact and clubhead speed, he can then work for added control in the backswing. Perfecting the backswing to a solid, orthodox position is virtually synonymous with strengthening the left arm and developing left-side control. There should be no mystery about the backswing and there are no short cuts to its perfection. A daily or weekly ritual of swinging the club with the left arm alone from address to the top of the backswing, holding it a moment, and then

Tom Watson's backswing, left side dominant, with the left shoulder turning, not dipping, and the plane of the left arm higher than the shoulder plane. The hands and wrists will *feel* active right from the moment of takeaway, more active than is apparent to the viewer

returning it to address as slowly as possible and as many times as possible will groove the movement. The left arm must be made to dominate the backswing and change of directions at the top of the swing. It must then learn to get out of the way and allow the right one to generate its power quite freely.

The attack

Having reached the top of the backswing, the player should then concentrate on attacking the ball and swinging on through to a balanced and poised followthrough. The change of directions at the top of the backswing is one of the most important moments in the golf swing, and one where all sorts of errors can creep in. In order to explain what should happen in the change of directions, it is now time to look at the way in which the ball is actually attacked.

The power in the golf swing through the impact zone is generated very largely with the right hand. The right hand and wrist are set into a crucial position in the backswing, with the right hand cocked back on itself so that the back of the hand and the forearm form a right angle. As the wrists cock in the backswing, with the left arm and hand dominant, the right hand should naturally fall into this position where the wrist is back on itself. As far as the right hand is concerned, any thoughts of the wrist cock should be centred on this hinging back of the right hand, not of the way, if any, in which the hand hinges up in the direction of the thumb. Power in the golf swing is generated by releasing the right hand from this fully cocked-back position so that the clubhead is virtually thrown

Left: Tom Weiskopf showing a classic backswing, club shaft horizontal and pointing directly down the target line, left arm and club face parallel and the right elbow forming a nice, neat right angle

Graham Marsh at various stages of the back and throughswing. Notice in particular the tremendous thrust backwards in the left leg as it firms up through impact

at the ball. In order to produce maximum distance the right hand is kept cocked back on itself in the downswing until the moment when the hand is released to throw the clubhead through the ball. To this end, the start of the downswing needs to be initiated with the left hand and left arm in control. The right hand and right shoulder are relatively passive in the start of the downswing, resisting any temptation to push forwards from the potentially powerful position they adopt at the top of the backswing.

A vital concept in the throughswing is the relative movements of the clubhead and right shoulder. The clubhead must travel from the top of the backswing right through and then over the left shoulder in a complete circle, while the right shoulder merely travels round through fifteen inches or so; emphasis must therefore be placed on swinging the *clubhead*, using the legs and leaving the right shoulder in a somewhat passive role as the downswing is initiated. It is crucial to swing the left arm *away* from the right shoulder. The majority of right-handed golfers tend to thrust force into the swing with the right side of the body so that the potential hit in the right hand and speed in the clubhead are usually dissipated before impact. Again it is a question of blending left and right correctly and producing left-side control where needed.

In order to obtain the correct movement of the right hand, the player often needs to have a feeling of hitting from the 'inside' just before impact. If you visualize the path of the clubhead

as it approaches and leaves the impact zone, as seen from above, the clubhead should be travelling on a curve, approaching the club from the inside, striking the ball and then returning again on to the inside. If there is any tendency to force the right shoulder and upper body into the shot, the body will tend to turn prematurely, bringing the clubhead into the ball from the outside – which as a rule sets the player up to pull the ball left of target or to start it left of target and slice it away to the right. To encourage the correct direction through impact it is necessary to visualize the correct curve to the clubhead path. The player then needs to concentrate very firmly on making the clubhead travel in this path as it approaches and leaves impact. As you attack the ball the feeling should be of the left hand and arm pulling down, setting the club to attack the ball from the inside. The right hand then releases the clubhead to square up the clubface at the very moment the ball is struck. The feeling needs to be 'Down with the left, then throw out with the right.' The looser and freer are the hands and wrists, the more likely you are to square up the clubface at impact or even fractionally before impact. By contrast, any tension in the hands and wrists tends to immobilize them and thus square up the clubface fractionally late, leaving it open at impact and producing a shot that slices away to the right.

In order to encourage the exact direction through impact it is helpful to have an idea of a spot on the ground perhaps twelve or eighteen

Ken Brown attacking the ball 'from the inside', right wrist cocked back ready to throw the clubhead out at the ball through impact

John Morgan showing the correct 'late hit', attacking the ball on a curved inside path with the clubhead behind the hands as it approaches impact

inches ahead of the ball and to focus your attention on driving the ball out over this spot so that it starts on target. An excellent exercise is to place a small coin on the ground just ahead of the ball and then to concentrate on starting the ball over this target, preferably having someone sitting behind you monitoring your accuracy in starting the ball on target. Make the ball travel on target for the first yard and your first aspect of direction is achieved. On the other hand, an inch out in the first fifteen is a ten-yard error at 150 yards.

As far as the mechanics of the swing are concerned, the important points in attacking the ball are to transfer the weight back from the ball of the left foot on to the heel of the left foot and to give the right foot and leg plenty of freedom, enabling the right foot to spin right through on to the tips of the toes by the end of the swing. If the leg action is initiated correctly with a thrust backwards into the left heel and freedom in the right foot, the centre and lower half of the body will turn through freely, encouraging the swing to move on target. Any tendency towards having the legs static either blocks the turning of the body so that the whole

shot is aimed to the right of target, or alternatively throws power and force into the shoulders so that the shoulders are swung round prematurely, pulling the clubhead off line quite sharply.

The key to the downswing and attack is therefore to keep the left arm in control, to push the weight back on to the left heel and to attack the ball from the inside, hitting hard with the right hand to square up the clubface at impact.

Finish and balance

Since the backswing is treated as purely preparatory to the throughswing, it is vital to concentrate your attention very largely on the end of the swing rather than the backswing. *It is crucial that you repeatedly practise the part of the swing beyond the ball to train yourself to adopt the correct position at the end of the swing.* For the long-handicap golfer it may almost mean that in striking the ball you must have the feeling of swinging to your natural followthrough and then correcting it into the right position. Obviously at first this will have no bearing on what

happens to the ball, for by the time you are making the correction the ball is well on its way. But what it does mean is that you are gradually learning to swing the club into a suitable position, even if the movement is initially somewhat artificial. In time the movements blend together to produce a satisfactory followthrough.

What you should see at the end of a perfect followthrough is that the right foot has spun round on to the tips of the toes, allowing the hips to turn through to the target, with the hands up high just beside the left ear, both arms bent, the wrists relaxed and the club hanging loosely down the back. The essentials are looseness in the wrists and freedom in the feet and legs. What is most important about the throughswing is that the movements become entirely free. There should never be any feeling of getting in the way of yourself, whether through restricted leg action, or because the left arm is rigid beyond impact, or through a swing that threatens to hit the player on the back of the head!

None of the movements involved in the throughswing is particularly difficult. Certainly, once there is sufficient control in the left arm in the backswing and change of directions at the top of the swing, most other difficulties are purely ones of understanding rather than physical strength or ability. In simple terms, the body turns through to face the target while the arms swing down and up to the other side. A good golf swing is largely a question of timing these two movements together. Most problems for the club golfer arise from turning the upper body – not the legs – while leaving the arms and clubhead behind. For the professional golfer and the player who hooks the ball the problem is more likely to be one of slowness in the body and legs. Timing is crucial.

The one movement that is perhaps difficult is the action of the left leg. At the top of the backswing, weight should be concentrated forward on the ball of the left foot, and pressure should be off the left heel even if it doesn't physically lift off the ground. In the downswing, weight must be thrust back into the heel and the left leg must be allowed to twist in the

Above: Bill Rogers in a classic followthrough, left leg firm, having spun freely through onto the toes of the right foot, hips facing the target. Any restriction in the foot action would inhibit the turning through of the body
Right: Tony Jacklin, with the left leg clearly twisting in the followthrough to enable him to turn through to the target. This freedom in the left leg is often one of the hardest movements for the club golfer to achieve. Without it the throughswing is inhibited

Above: Tom Watson en route to a followthrough with the club pointing almost directly away from the target. Both arms are clearly folding up together to maintain the target-line for as long as possible beyond impact

Left: Beyond impact the left arm must be allowed to fold smoothly inwards, with the elbows remaining comparatively close. This helps keep the club travelling on-target beyond impact for reliability and consistency through impact

throughswing so that the hips can face the target. The correct followthrough would in fact be entirely simple if it were not for the position of the left foot. All the followthrough amounts to is the whole body facing towards the target with both arms folded, hands by the left ear and the club draped over the left shoulder. If you start by facing your target with your feet together and simply put the right foot out into its correct position behind you, you will see how simple this is. Doing the whole thing at speed with the left foot in the same position as it was at address means that the left leg has to be pulled back under the body, twisting through to the target so that the foot and hips point in different directions. This is a question of loosening up the left leg, giving it freedom and enabling it to twist into the right position.

Although the left side must be dominant in the backswing and start of the downswing, it must be trained to fold out of the way smoothly just beyond impact to give the right hand freedom to generate power. Just as the right arm folded away in the backswing, so the left one must fold away in the throughswing. Many golfers labour under the misapprehension that the left arm must be rigid at impact. This is the case with certain punch shots but not with the full, flowing swing. The left arm must be allowed to fold inwards – not break outwards – beyond impact. Correctly the club should therefore move out towards the target and, at a point where the clubhead is perhaps knee-high, both arms must be allowed to fold up so that the clubhead moves directly up and over the left shoulder, following the general direction of the target.

Here again we have a problem which mainly stems from the two-handed game. Both arms cannot and should not stay straight for very many inches beyond impact. This could physically happen only if the right shoulder dropped unsatisfactorily or if the shoulders turned prematurely towards the target. The right arm remains straight for a little longer than the left but there must be a point at which the arms fold up in order to maintain the target line. Don't have any feeling of exaggeratedly pushing the club out towards the target or keeping it particularly low to the ground in a mistaken search for 'width'. Swing the clubhead through the ball and then allow the arms to fold up. In this way the clubhead can be kept travelling very much on target. *A followthrough where the club points back and away from the target is as indicative of good direction as is a backswing that is perfectly on target.* Both demonstrate the overall line of the swing and help to produce consistency.

In the correct followthrough everything should be perfectly balanced so that the end of the swing is controlled despite the speed of the action. You can afford to swing as fast as possible through the ball only if the balance is perfect. The player who is told that he swings too fast is usually not really guilty of producing too much speed – after all, maximum speed in the clubhead is one of the prime objects of the swing – but is probably merely guilty of bad footwork and poor balance. If you produce perfect balance you can swing the clubhead as fast and hard as you like through impact without any danger of going off line.

Most golfers don't produce maximum clubhead speed. It isn't generally through lack of strength, but rather through lack of freedom in the throughswing. They put the brakes on through impact instead of letting the clubhead move. This is because the followthrough isn't grooved into being free. The player gets in the way of himself and subconsciously feels that a really full, free swing could crack him on the back of the head. He daren't let rip. In the correctly developed followthrough the arms swing out towards the target, fold up freely, and the club shaft whips back over the left shoulder, hands clear of the head. All of a sudden the player knows where he is going, loses his inhibitions and begins to revel in the feeling of freedom, blended with the necessary modicum of control.

If you look at almost all really top-class professionals, you will see that the end of their swing is perfectly poised and looks as though they mean business. *A good followthrough is* not *the result of a good shot and a good swing. The fact is that* thinking *of producing a good followthrough and aiming the whole swing at getting itself into this position is really the* cause *of a good shot.* Try to swing the club from the top of the backswing

Above: Bobby Clampett shows a followthrough in which the club swings over and away from the target, the club pointing almost directly back and behind him, *not* round and across behind the head

Above right: Nick Faldo, clubhead swinging through, up and over on line

into a perfect followthrough, a followthrough that you can hold for at least two or three seconds at the end of the swing; you will find that this eliminates almost all the really bad shots on the golf course. It will not guarantee that every shot is perfect – nothing can – but it does virtually guarantee for the majority of golfers that there is never a real disaster. One of the best exercises for training yourself to produce a really repetitive swing is to practise hitting full shots with a driver or with some other long club and to concentrate on holding the followthrough position until the ball has landed. If this is combined with hitting the ball as hard as possible it teaches the player to produce perfect control combined with maximum speed. The golfer should then take the

feeling of this exercise out on to the golf course, concentrating on holding the end of the swing for a count of two or three on every full shot – and indeed on every short shot. Soon the swing becomes more repetitive and the player starts to produce a solid swing with increasingly good results.

Thinking of a perfectly balanced full finish *causes* good shots. It is not the result of a good shot. Swing at maximum speed through the ball and train yourself to hold a balanced finish for at least three seconds. The better the balance, the better you will withstand pressure.

5 Imagination: The Destructive Negative and the Invisible Target

The various facets of the golfing mind all play their part in overall performance. Imagination is in some ways the most crucial aspect. *A well-trained imagination can be a tremendous asset; an imagination, particularly a vivid one, which runs away with itself can prove a disaster.* Perfect control of the imagination is absolutely vital for good scoring and tournament success. Imagination and imagery of a slightly different kind play their part in developing the swing and technical excellence.

The degree to which we use our imagination varies considerably from one individual to another. Some people can conjure up images in their mind which seem almost real, not only visual images but also images in the other senses. Others have little or no imaginative ability in one or all of the senses.

As we have seen earlier, the golfing mind is at its most receptive to the acquisition of physical skills through its facility for imitation. Attempting to learn, as most adults do, through a process of verbal self-instruction is far less productive and in many ways explains the difference in aptitude for adults and children in learning new physical tasks. Imagination is in many ways suppressed by conventional education and tends to take a very secondary role in thinking, as language and abstract thought develop. The use of imitation and visual imagery undoubtedly begins to deteriorate – or at least be less utilized – in adulthood. The particularly creative individual and those who perform certain skills to a high level usually appear to retain vivid imaginative ability in the appropriate sense. The virtuoso musician can as a rule imagine the whole of the concerto from

start to finish, presumably sensing the feel of playing the particular instrument involved and no doubt imagining the overall sensation of a public performance. The trained athlete almost always has a high degree of movement imagery, not only enabling him to imagine his own movements, but also making it very possible to watch someone else's movements and to 'feel' himself performing the same actions.

When trying to develop his swing technique, the golfer needs to utilize his imaginative ability as far as possible in order to picture the movements he wants to copy and mentally to put himself into these movements. His learning of the overall swing shape through imitation – and ultimately perhaps through role-playing – is highly dependent on the faculty of imagination.

Imagery and muscle memory

The more you play golf – or any sport, for that matter – the more the movements used become engrained in the mind and body. Sheer repetition of a certain movement means that each such repetition strengthens the pattern of behaviour, like adding an additional wire to a cable, until the particular pattern of movement is fully established and hard to break. This is the way habits are formed and physical skills grooved. Continuous repetition of swinging a golf club builds up a pattern of movement that is reinforced with every practice session. If the movements are correct, practice is beneficial in developing consistency, but if faulty it then takes time to break down the movement

Purely imagining the movements of the
swing can act to strengthen muscle memory
and increase the likelihood of repetition in
the swing

patterns before renewing them with strands of a different behaviour 'cable'.

What the golfer may not appreciate is that the powers of the imagination can be so great that purely imagining the movements without any physical activity can act to strengthen the muscle-memory pattern. Contemplating any recent instruction or practice, imagining as vividly as possible the *feelings* of the movements, undoubtedly consolidates the desired sensations. Purely and simply thinking about and imagining a physical task strengthens the behaviour pattern and makes it all the more likely for that particular movement to take place. As we shall see later, this use of mental rehearsal can be used systematically in improving overall performance.

With experience the player develops an enormous wealth of muscle-memory traces which enables him to play every shot quite naturally. In playing a small-pitch shot, for example, the player looks at the flag and takes in the whole impression of the situation facing him – the slope, weather conditions, distance, and so on. He doesn't have the problems the beginner has of not knowing how far to swing the club or how hard to strike the ball to produce the desired shot. What happens in time is that the player acquires the ability to be able to look at a specific shot and simply by looking at that shot tune the brain into the correct muscle-memory programme so that the body in turn responds with the correct movement. The top-class player when pitching a ball reaches the point where he only has to look at the target – say, 8o yards away – and this visual input acts as a very refined tuning process which sets him into the programme for an 8o-yard-pitch shot. He needs virtually no additional linguistic input. Similarly, he may want to fade a drive into a certain position or to play a low punching shot. His body responds very quickly to the picture and feel of the shot he wants to produce, allowing

In time the good player acquires the ability to look at any shot, the brain takes it all in very quickly and 'tunes in' to the correct muscle-memory programme to produce the shot very reliably. Judging shots becomes quite instinctive

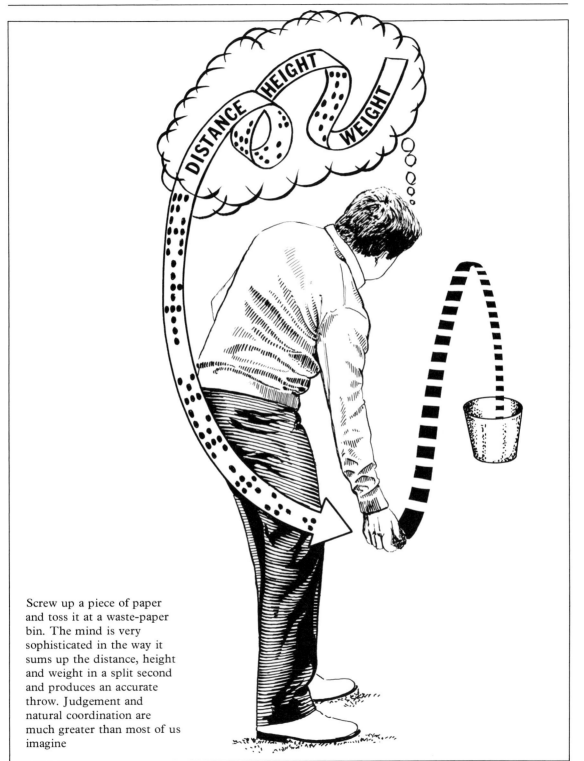

Screw up a piece of paper and toss it at a waste-paper bin. The mind is very sophisticated in the way it sums up the distance, height and weight in a split second and produces an accurate throw. Judgement and natural coordination are much greater than most of us imagine

him to move easily into the correct set-up position, but also gearing the muscles almost subconsciously to work in the correct way and to blend together naturally.

Even for the club golfer this kind of muscle-memory tracing is probably far more sophisticated than the player imagines. Turning to a non-golf task, imagine yourself tossing a screwed-up piece of paper into a waste-paper basket. With even a modicum of experience at this, the reasonably well-coordinated person can merely look at the target and make a pretty good or even accurate attempt at tossing the paper into the bin. The body's mental and physical abilities are so much greater than the majority of us appreciate that what is actually happening in this very simple task is that there is a subconscious assessment of distance, height, weight of the missile, and so on, all of which are juggled around by a highly sophisticated inner mechanism which usually produces a very adequate result. The missile-tossing memory trace is indeed quite well developed in most of us without any formal training or practice.

In golf the majority of players with some experience at the game generally have a much greater bank of muscle-memory programmes than they imagine. Indeed, most golfers would perform at a very much higher level if they would just look at the target involved, trust their very sophisticated mental processes to do the rest and simply get on with the swing. A lot of club golfers allow this to happen relatively freely once they are on the green. They manage to putt fairly accurately, merely by looking at the hole and allowing the body to coordinate fairly freely to produce the right weight and length of shot. As a rule they don't force themselves into swinging the putter back and through a certain distance but seem to appreciate that 'it just happens'. By giving the body and mind freedom in the same way in the long game they would almost certainly find that the same effect resulted. The mind would go through its own process of assessing the situation, slotting into the correct swing programme and thereby assisting the player to do his very best. Trying too hard results in an over-

analytical assessment of the situation – which in turn suppresses the muscle memory.

> **Repetition, whether physical or mental, of the golf swing builds up a muscle-memory programme, i.e. it is habit-forming. With experience, merely looking at the target or visualizing the flight of the desired shot keys the body into the correct set of movements.**

Visual imagery and positive thinking

Muscle memory is one of the greatest weapons for the good golfer, enabling him to play a full repertoire of shots with relative ease. This must sound marvellous to the club golfer. However, it does have its drawbacks.

The destructive negative

The great danger for both the club golfer and the professional is to get some kind of negative idea in the mind. Players very often stand on a tee, look down the fairway and then think to themselves: 'Whatever I do I mustn't slice into those trees.' Alternatively, the player may be saying: 'Help, help. I drove out of bounds yesterday. Please don't let me do the same thing today.'

What the player is doing is falling into the common trap of giving himself a set of negative commandments. This is quite disastrous. If you think of something like the flight of a golf ball, where movement is concerned, this is almost always linked to a pictorial image. For some people this image is going to be clearer than for others, and for the relatively experienced golfer is likely to be quite vivid. As we have just seen, experience with the game leads to a building up of the muscle-memory store so that visual input keys the player in to the appropriate pattern of movement. It is not possible to visualize some-

It is important for all thoughts to be positive. The images in your mind become a set of instructions. If you think of what you *don't* want to do – in this case to slice – you will picture just the thing you are trying to avoid. This picture acts as an instruction and you are likely to produce the wretched slice you wanted to avoid

thing that is negative. *If you say to yourself, 'What I must* not *do is to slice the ball', the visual image in your brain is of a slice.* In other words, you are going to visualize exactly the same thing whether you are telling yourself to slice or *not* to slice. *What in fact happens is that the image you are conjuring up of the slice – the very thing you do not want to produce – acts as a form of instruction to your mind and muscles and therefore encourages the wretched slice you wanted to avoid.*

To a certain extent this kind of imagery is more important for the low-handicap or top-class golfer. He will respond rather more to the instructions he gives himself and can virtually hook or slice the ball at will, without making any really noticeable changes in technique. He merely has to think of the way in which he wants the ball to bend. If all the images remain positive, then this can work for him. But on the other hand, if he allows the wrong kind of thought to creep into the mind, then a negative thought will act as his instruction and produce the very shot he did not want. Most top-class golfers will produce a really bad shot on the golf course only if they cannot get the right picture of the shot they are trying to produce. Under competitive pressure the ability to produce the right kind of picture sometimes tends to be inhibited and the golfer may find it almost impossible to cut out the pictures of the shots he wants to avoid.

For the club golfer it is still absolutely vital to produce the right kind of *positive* image of the shot you want to produce. If faced with a little shot over a bunker and on to the green, you must have an image in your mind of the type of action and type of shot you are trying to produce. It is absolutely no use standing behind the bunker and imagining the ball dribbling along the ground. If you imagine this you will give yourself the wrong set of instructions and your muscle memory will do its very best to trickle the ball into the sand! Exactly the same thing can happen with a short putt. If you imagine a ball being dragged away to the left, you will drag it away to the left. If, on the other hand, you can train yourself to think of the ball diving into the hole, you have every chance of sinking the putt.

The destructive negative

An examination of learning skills and difficulties will lead the golfing mind to realize that the use of words as instructions is relatively fruitless in acquiring a physical skill. The well-trained golfing mind will begin to see the value of adopting a childlike, imitative approach to learning where pictures are the keys. In time the images in the mind become the instructions on which the brain and body react. The uninitiated golfer is generally hampered by use of negative images of what he wants to avoid. The negative requirement is missed out and the brain and body tune into just the shot the player wants to avoid – the destructive negative.

Practice and play

The use of imagery and imagination of this kind is very often the key to enabling the player to perform at his best on the golf course. There are three distinct stages in learning to become a good golfer. The first stage is to learn to swing the club in a practice swing in a reasonably smooth and technically correct way. The second stage is one of learning to swing the club with exactly the same technique when faced with the ball. The third stage is to be able to take that same swing out on to the golf course and to make it stand up to all sorts of competitive pressure. Many golfers reach the stage of swinging the club in a fairly orthodox manner and producing reasonably good results on the practice ground, but then find it almost impossible to strike the ball as well on the golf course. Frequently this kind of player becomes frustrated at the game because no amount of tuition on the practice ground ever seems to produce improved results on the golf course. The most basic problem for the kind of golfer who is an

YES

NO

It is essential at all times to have a positive image of where you are trying to go and *never* what you are trying to avoid

under-achiever on a golf course is that he simply does not think correctly when playing, as opposed to when practising. Lack of use of one aspect of imagery is the key to certain failures; letting the imagination run away with itself is the key to others.

The brain and body need some kind of input to tell them what to do. There need to be two kinds of input. The first is the purely visual input of the target you are trying to hit, combined with a vivid picture of the flight of the desired shot. This should be sufficient to key the experienced golfer into producing the right kind of swing. In other words, it switches on the right programme in the muscle-memory store.

As a second input there needs to be a very definite rehearsal of the movements involved. The good golfer will usually picture the flight of the shot required, go through a swift mental rehearsal of the movements and in this way be able to produce the same thing with the ball. Many club golfers fail to give themselves any such kind of instruction. First of all, they probably have no real mental picture of the target. Second, they probably do not imagine the desired flight of the ball and, third, they almost certainly do not mentally rehearse the actions.

During practice the very fact of hitting one shot after another tends to tune the brain and body into the right kind of movement. By hitting one shot after another the player is building up a pattern of movements. Once out on the golf course it is quite different, for what you obviously have to do is produce the correct shot *once* and once alone. You do not get numerous tries and you do not have the advantage of a build-up of repetition.

What you should be doing in playing every golf shot is first to visualize the way in which you want the ball to fly and, second, to produce a kind of mental dress rehearsal which gives your brain the necessary instructions for making the right swing. Whether or not you have a physical practice swing – something I would highly recommend – it is essential to prepare your brain and muscles for the kind of movement involved.

The second reason why players are so frequently under-achievers on the golf course is that they adopt an entirely different approach to striking the ball. On the driving range they are probably faced with a wide-open space, with no particular pressure to strike a target. The mind will probably either be focused on the technique to be developed or be concentrated in a relatively relaxed way on the flag. Once you get out on to the golf course there are all kinds of distractions and extra difficulties to cope with. Instead of focusing on the target and simply thinking of striking the ball from A to B as on the driving range, the player is probably not so much thinking of B as thinking 'Please, not C, or D, or E. . . .' He begins to see all the problem areas and distractions and instead of concentrating on a positive target falls into the trap of negative thinking. He probably ceases to become target-oriented and thinks in an entirely different way from during practice. He should be thinking 'Here I am, trying to make the best-looking swing I can and trying to hit this wretched ball from A to B.' Instead, this is probably the very last thing in his mind and he is by now worrying about who is watching, imagining what is going to go wrong with the shots and generally thinking about all manner of things apart from the task in hand.

One of the best ways of improving a player's ability round the golf course is to train him to think out loud and relate exactly what is going on in his mind prior to striking the ball. Most people are initially slightly inhibited at doing this and require a certain amount of prompting from their coach. It soon becomes apparent, however, that very many of their thoughts are totally destructive, as far as playing round the course is concerned.

> **If you are a player whose standard in practice is far higher than in play, or if you deteriorate under pressure, talk out loud to yourself in order to reveal the destructive, negative thoughts which are probably impeding performance.**

In practising, hitting one shot after another grooves the swing and a pattern of movements is built up. On the golf course this is very different. The task is to produce the correct shot just once. It is necessary to visualize the shot wanted and to have a kind of mental dress rehearsal of the swing to be produced

3 Shots to win

Controlling the mental situation

Almost all golfers are aware of changed desires and emotions, combined with a different level of performance, in various situations. Their responses vary according to whether they are actually playing or merely practising, and whether they are under pressure or not. There may be a serious deterioration in technique from practice to actual play; there may be a total breakdown of technique during particularly pressurized tournaments.

It is vital to appreciate that the *physical* task of striking the ball to a target remains exactly the same on the practice ground, on the golf course, in a friendly game and under the most severe championship conditions. The task is one of striking the ball from the spot on the ground in front of you to the target x yards away. The only thing that alters according to practice, play or pressure is the mental state of the player. The only change is within the mind. This is where perfect control of concentration and imagination is absolutely essential to optimum performance.

The golfer who competes at any level must be made aware of his own responses to a changed mental situation. The golfer needs to analyse his own performance and inner thoughts in three situations – practice, play and pressure. In practice, his degree of reliability with certain shots may be relatively high. His technique may be adequate and his thoughts uncluttered and productive. For many players the pattern of thought then changes quite dramatically as soon as they begin actually to play, and this results in a deterioration of technique. The pressure of competition may produce a quite different pattern of thought and in turn lead to a disintegration of the swing. Other players – a tiny percentage – thrive on pressure, perform less well under ordinary playing conditions and are at their worst in practice. Whichever way the player reacts, whether thriving on or suffering under pressure, the three situations each produce a different mental approach and with it varying performance.

The serious player needs to go through a period of searching introspection, developing a full awareness of his productive or destructive thoughts and worries. 'What thoughts cloud my mind in a competition? Do I become careful or worry? How does my mental approach to a 5-iron shot differ on the practice ground from the last hole of the championship?' Having analysed the type of thoughts and mental states that bring out the best and the worst in the individual, he then needs to learn to control the mental situation through his imagination to encourage the correct pattern of thinking.

If a player performs particularly well on the practice ground, then he needs to retain the illusion that he is still on the practice ground when he is playing or under pressure. If he strikes the ball reliably on a practice ground, aiming at a white post or umbrella, or whatever, then he needs to go out on to the golf course and mentally put himself into that very same situation. He needs to be able to create in his mind that particular feeling and routine, however much pressure he is under. He may well be advised to practise continually on the driving range or on the practice ground to a set target so that the image of striking a ball to this target becomes deeply engrained in his mind. He can then go on the course but still 'see' himself as being on the practice ground, aiming at his same target and still 'being' in a practice situation. This ability can without doubt be enhanced by mental rehearsal, sitting and relaxing and simply visualizing himself in the situation at which his performance level is highest.

The player needs to rehearse conjuring up the picture of standing on the practice ground, with his target, so that this very vivid picture can always be produced if necessary when under pressure, in order to create in the player's mind the feeling of a relaxed, practice situation. In this way the player should be able to produce the correct thoughts of the physical task in hand rather than being sidetracked into worrying or trying too hard.

The person who either doesn't practise or certainly finds himself performing better during relaxed play needs to take that mental state into his competitive games. He needs to be

The physical task of hitting a golf ball remains the same on the practice ground, in play or under pressure. The task is to hit the ball from a spot on the ground in front of you to a target x yards away. The only change is the mental state of the player. This needs to be understood and controlled

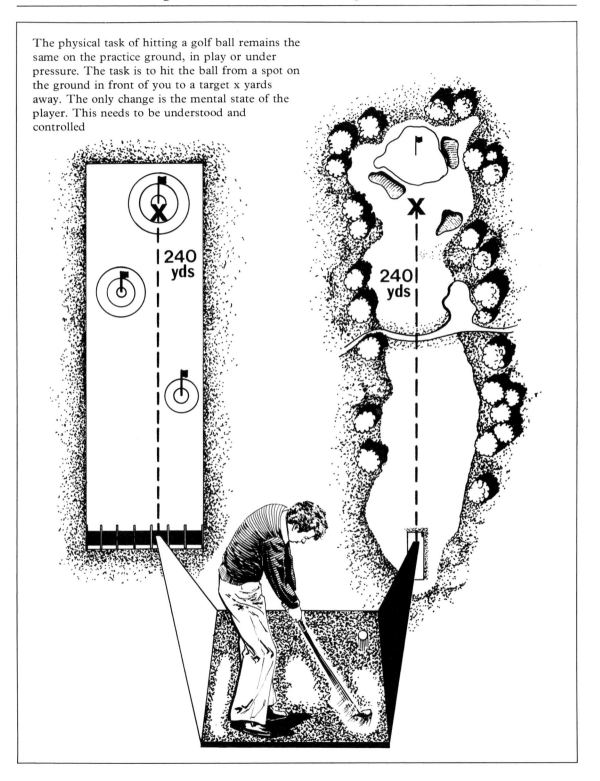

PRESSURE

The player who is better in practice than under pressure needs to take the illusion that he is still on the practice ground out into his playing and pressure situations. He needs to conjure up a vivid picture of the practice situation, complete with imaginary target, to keep his mind firmly on the physical task in hand rather than being sidetracked into worrying

able to concentrate and imagine himself still playing a friendly game, playing a few holes while exercising the dog or, indeed, whatever brings out the best in his own particular game. Again it is a question of controlling the mind, mentally rehearsing the desired situation and then being able to concentrate on reproducing that to control the mental situation.

The vast majority of players deteriorate under competitive conditions. The fault is simply that they are trying too hard and are thereby creating a form of pressure which is not compatible with good golf. The more relaxed and carefree you can be about the game, the better you will generally perform. Any tendency to put yourself under the pressure of saying 'I *must* do well' usually inhibits the mental processes, tightens up the muscles and leads to a lowering of performance. The body may begin to function completely differently, pumping through excess adrenaline or tightening the muscles. The whole essence of mental control is one of being able to create your own situation. You are not in a championship. You are not playing for large amounts of money. You are hitting the ball from A to B on your practice ground. It doesn't matter what happens. This shot is for the Open Championship. This putt is for a million dollars. The mental situation is your own making.

Mental rehearsal

To a certain extent you may learn through experience to control your thoughts and emotions, producing the illusion of a situation in which you thrive. Systematic mental rehearsal of the desired circumstances is an important and serious weapon for the aspiring sports performer. Use of this type of mental technique, particularly in eastern Europe, has led to such improvement in competitive performance that many sportsmen use a rigorous form of mental rehearsal of this type in their training programme. In many instances the process of mental rehearsal of the whole task is so vivid that it brings about the changes in the body functions that one might expect in the physical situation. The rate of heartbeat probably increases and the level of adrenaline alters. There may be changes in the breathing pattern, muscular tension, temperature, and so on. The athlete can thereby attune himself for both the external and the internal experience. Through this process, the top-class sportsman gradually learns control of his body functions by producing the desired thoughts. He may begin to appreciate what kind of thinking produces excessive adrenaline or establishes the correct arousal level.

For the golfer, very much the same applies. In some ways, because of the time permitted for over-analysing, mental rehearsal and mental control are almost more important. The player may need to train himself to be totally phlegmatic when he is under pressure or he may need to create the illusion of pressure where none exists. Every competitive golfer does this to some extent, but the rehearsal may be unsystematic and therefore relatively fruitless. He probably thinks about what is likely to happen the next day, what he hopes for and what he worries about. He needs to channel these thoughts into productive mental practice. He needs to practise not only the physical swing he is going to produce the next day on a certain tee, but also the thought that will precede and accompany that swing. Not only does he need to think about needing a four for the Open Championship; he needs to rehearse over and over again the thoughts that will enable him to carry that through to the best of his ability.

The situation that brings out the best in you may well not be the same situation as brings out the best in your playing partner, your professional or in me. But, on the whole, perhaps 99 per cent of golfers perform at their best with *all* pressure removed. It is therefore important to assess your own optimum mental state and to rehearse reproducing it as thoroughly as possible. The technique of controlling the mental situation merely requires concentration and a degree of practice in a quiet moment.

Similarly, you may have particular shots that you like or don't like, drives from certain tees which seem very much more difficult than drives from other tees. Once again the answer is to control your own mental state. If you like

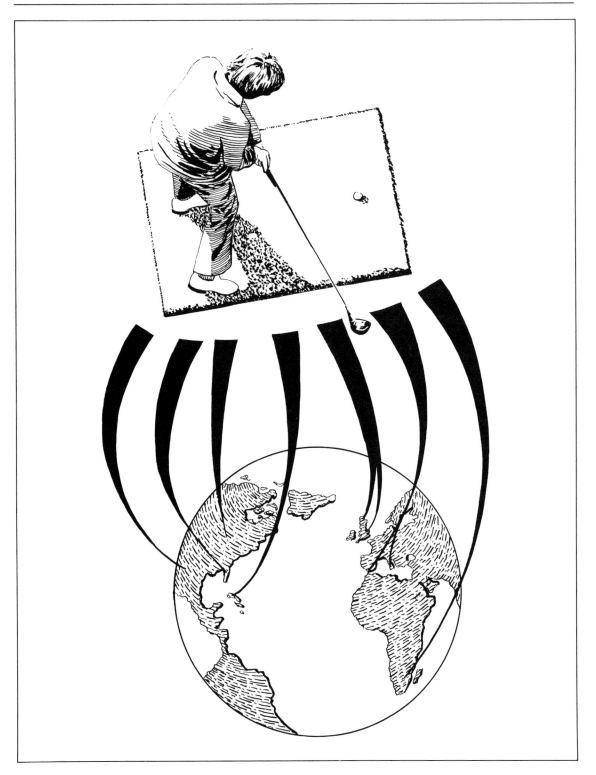

driving from the tenth tee on the Old Course at Sunningdale more than you like driving from the seventeenth tee at St Andrews, then mentally whisk yourself away from one to the other. You have to create the illusion and if necessary imagine you are somewhere completely different from reality. If you have a particular drive you like and generally perform well, keep visualizing yourself in this situation until you can always take that round with you to use when the physical circumstances are not to your liking.

After all, you are simply teeing up the ball and standing on a square of flat ground, and that square of flat ground is precisely the same whenever and wherever in the world you happen to be. *If*, that is, you acquire sufficient mental control.

For the longer-handicap player, wherever there is a golfing situation you don't like, change it! If you don't want to be hitting over a pond or over a bunker or between forests of trees, change the situation to one that brings out the best in your golf. See yourself as being on the practice ground, aiming at an umbrella or white post, or whatever.

The physical task in golf is simply one of striking the ball from A to B. For most people, what gets in the way of hitting a ball from A to B repeatedly are the adverse pictures and situations in the brain which inhibit optimum performance.

> **Try to determine the practice–play– pressure situation at which you perform best and control the mental situation by mastering your imagination. Practise conjuring up pictures of specific shots or positions you enjoy and take these out on to the golf course with you to ward off negative thoughts.**

The value of mental routine

Almost all top-class golfers go through a set routine in their approach to each shot. You can see clearly that they always position the caddie in an identical place, adopt the address position in a systematic way, produce the same mannerisms of adjusting a glove or trouser leg, and so on, and in this way enable themselves to produce a repetitive swing. What the championship golfer usually manages to do is produce a thoroughly systematic and routine *mental* approach in playing each shot. He assesses the whole situation, the target, the club required, the weather conditions, and so on. He then focuses his mind on the task in hand and meticulously picks out one or two points of his technique upon which to concentrate. Any weakness in the shots of the championship golfer almost always arises when his mind wanders off at this stage and suffers minor distractions. The truly world-class golfer overcomes this through a repetitive, step-by-step thought process in setting up to the ball and executing the shot.

The club golfer, by contrast, usually has no set physical routine to approaching each shot, let alone a repetitive mental one. He probably positions his clubs in a totally random way, assesses the situation fairly haphazardly and probably fails to isolate his thoughts on technique in a logical and chronological order. In this way his mind is not perfectly focused and tends to be distracted into unproductive thinking.

There are two essential points in the mental run-up to striking the ball. The first is to become as repetitive as possible in the thoughts about the physical task in hand, the technique of the swing and the aim and object of the shot. By doing this the player establishes every key thought for the swing in chronological order,

Facing page: If there is a golfing situation you don't like, learn to change it mentally. Imagine you are playing a particular hole or shot you do like. Try to control the mental situation so that you can isolate your thoughts to the ball, the square of ground you and the ball are positioned on, and forget everything else around you except for the target. Imagine your favourite golf hole or tee shot and 'take' that square of ground with you wherever you play

confines his thoughts to a set time period and avoids mentally wandering off into over-analysing and worrying. The second point concerns target awareness.

The invisible target

Not only is it essential to choose a positive target as the aim of every shot but it is essential to be able to picture this target throughout the shot. In setting up to the shot you should, of course, be setting your feet and your whole body in the correct direction to strike the ball on target. This in itself does not produce sufficient control for you to hit the ball perfectly straight. Unless you have some overall concept of the desired direction of the shot, the line of the approach into the ball will lack sufficient accuracy. You need to have either a marked spot on the ground perhaps eighteen inches in front of the ball to aim over or else a perfect picture of the target in your mind's eye so that you know where you are trying to strike the ball. Preferably you should have both.

What is crucial in the pre-shot routine is that you develop the ability to be able to look at the target, look back at the ball and yet retain a very vivid picture of that target throughout the remainder of the swing. It is no good having just a vague idea of where you are striking the ball. Pick out the flag, or a definite tree or something on the horizon to aim at. If there isn't anything as specific as you require, then what you need to do is to imagine a target – a large bull's-eye, a flag, etc. – exactly where you want to aim. You need to be able to address the ball and retain this image as perfectly as possible. Not only does this apply in the long game but, as we shall see later, it applies just as much in the short game.

Unless you have a perfect mental picture of your target throughout the shot, the tendency is almost always one of looking up too soon in a vain attempt to see the ball and the target within the space of vision at the same time. Although in most ball games you should be looking at the ball at the moment of impact, you generally also have the target in your field of vision, even if not perfectly defined and in focus. It is relatively

unusual in other games for the player to have to be totally aware of a target behind him or beyond his peripheral vision, and certainly not such a small target at such a great distance. In golf, this is essential at all times. Only on the shortest of putts can one truly see the ball and the hole at the same time. The player who finds it difficult to imagine the target throughout the shot needs mentally to rehearse conjuring up the physical target or imagining a purely mental one. Without this, there is an overriding tendency to look up too soon or there is likely to be a severe problem with direction.

In golf you cannot see the target and ball at the same time. It is essential after looking at the target to retain a perfect mental picture of it so that you can concentrate on striking the ball on-target without the tendency to look up too soon to see ball and flag simultaneously

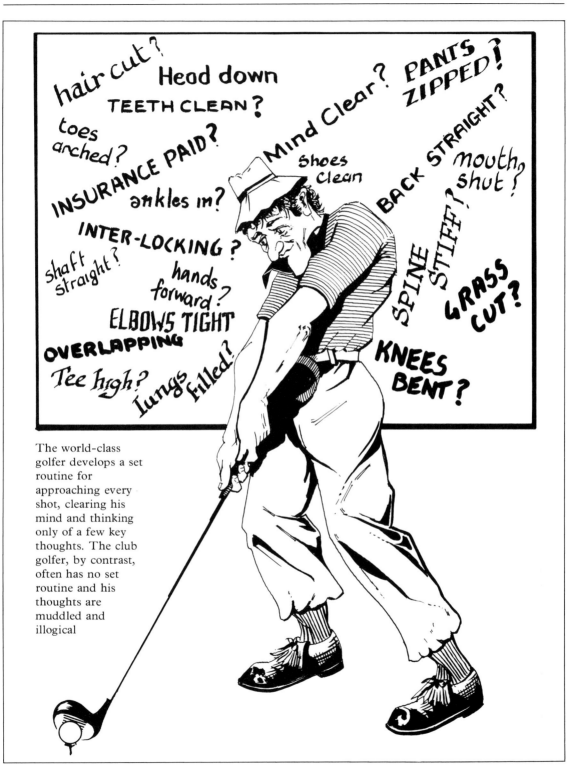

The world-class golfer develops a set routine for approaching every shot, clearing his mind and thinking only of a few key thoughts. The club golfer, by contrast, often has no set routine and his thoughts are muddled and illogical

What one again needs to bear in mind is that there are two aspects to direction. The first is the line in which the ball starts and the second is the way in which it curves. The player who can start the ball accurately on target usually finds relatively few problems around the golf course. Start the ball straight and any spin or curve is usually not too destructive. In order to set the ball off in the right direction it is essential to retain a vivid image of the target throughout the swing. Lose that image and your chances of starting the ball on target, let alone making it finish there, are relatively slim.

> **Develop good target awareness to overcome the problem of not being able to see ball and target together through impact. Create a vivid picture of the target in your pre-shot routine and concentrate firmly on starting every shot perfectly on this target.**

Developing imagery

Developing perfectly controlled imagery and imagination is one of the great assets for the trained golfing mind. As we have seen earlier in the chapter, imagination can be used to control the mental situation, relieve the stresses and strains of competition and also to slot the player into the right muscle-memory programme for producing the desired movements. The ability to conjure up images undoubtedly varies considerably from one individual to another. Some people have a highly developed visual imagination, others can control their auditory imagery to a great extent and others have a comparatively vague idea of what imagery really is. The player who is a good athlete and well coordinated almost certainly has an exceptional ability to develop movement imagery so that he can watch movement in others and interpret this into a feeling for his own movement. He can, in other words, put himself 'inside' another person and feel the movements involved.

For comparatively good golfers whose imaginative ability is distinctly limited, there is likely to be a certain limitation to their whole game. First, they are likely to find a change of technique a problem. They find it difficult to translate what they see into what they feel and in turn into what they do. Second, the person whose imagery level is relatively low usually finds it difficult to imagine the target sufficiently vividly and may find great difficulty in controlling the mental situation. On the other hand, the person whose imagination is relatively unused does not fall into the trap of allowing himself to be distracted by unnecessary thoughts of what might or might not happen.

Ability at imagery can almost certainly be improved. Psychological research has shown that active attempts to improve the process of imagery can bear fruit. The golfer who now realizes that his own use of imagery is relatively low would certainly do well to practise conjuring up images until the process develops and improves.

As a starting point, try fixing your attention on a specific object for perhaps ten or twelve seconds, then close your eyes and try to see a definite after-image of the object. This should be relatively simple. First of all the object was there, then you closed your eyes and the image should have remained. Now having obtained the after-image turn your head to the side and consider what happens. Either you will have turned your head to the side and your after-image will stay with the object, so that it is now in the corner of your visual space, or you will have taken the image with you and it will still be in the middle of your imagery vision. Now again concentrate on the object and develop the same kind of after-image with your eyes shut. Try to retain the picture for as long as you can and then as the picture gradually fades open your eyes and look back to the object again. Study the object fully until you are absolutely aware of all its little intricacies of construction. Then close your eyes and allow the after-image to develop. Having produced the after-image, now turn the object over in your mind. With your eyes still closed try to turn the object upside down. Imagine it lifting into the air, moving across to

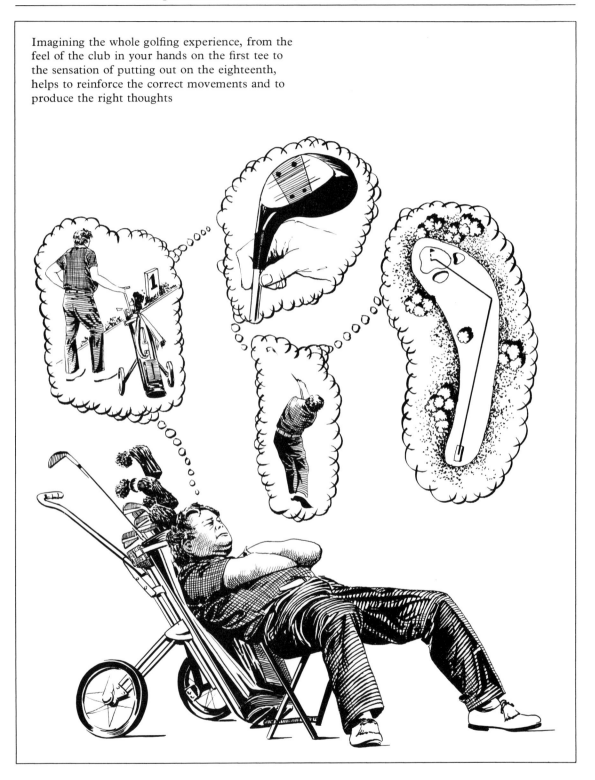

Imagining the whole golfing experience, from the feel of the club in your hands on the first tee to the sensation of putting out on the eighteenth, helps to reinforce the correct movements and to produce the right thoughts

the side perhaps four or five feet, and then make it land slowly on the ground. Now try to lift the object above the ground to perhaps four feet, hold it for perhaps five seconds and then let the object drop on to the ground and disintegrate. In this way you are beginning to have the feeling of imagery and also control of that imagery.

In order to develop the imagery sense in a golfing context try to take yourself out into a golfing situation. If your sense of imagery is not very good, then start with one basic set exercise which you keep repeating until your awareness and vividness of imagery gradually improves. Start by imagining yourself going out to play a round of golf on your own golf course. Again sit in a relaxed position, and you will probably find the imagery far easier if you close your eyes. Gradually you should find that you can conjure up images which become so strong that you can even do this with your eyes open, making your mental images override the physical world in front of you. Start by imagining yourself walking to the first tee, feeling yourself pulling your

trolley or carrying your bag and imagining the route to the first hole. Take out your driver, or whatever club you are likely to use, have a few practice swings and imagine that you are waiting for the people in front to get out of the way. Now go through the whole process of how you would play the first hole to the very best of your ability. This should be everything from the process of teeing up the ball, aiming the shot and so on right through the hole in the way you would like to play it. If this is relatively simple, then go on and do two or three more holes. Go through a definite pattern of imagining this process in your mind.

If you regularly mentally rehearse your golf for five minutes a day, you will soon find that the vividness of the situation grows. Perhaps the weather will change from one time to another. Perhaps you are playing with different people. Try to visualize the whole golfing environment – the sounds, smells, touch, and so on. Make your images as vivid and real as they would be in physical life. Gradually you should find that

Learn to produce the swing you want by picturing in your mind the golfer you want to copy. Try to retain an image of your example and slot into these movements with as little verbal analysis as possible

you begin to get a really vivid feeling of your own shots. You should be able to feel the strike of the ball, the way you contact the ground, the putt diving into the hole, and so on. Try to imagine the spring beneath your feet as you walk on thick, lush grass. Try to make the whole picture as vivid and pure as you can. And then from there gradually set yourself into different types of golfing situations. Imagine, if you like, Jack Nicklaus coming to play on your golf course. Imagine what he would do and how he would look and how he would feel and talk and walk. Try to sense the whole experience. Try to put yourself inside that type of movement until you gradually develop a real awareness of what the golf swing and the whole golf game feel like to him. If you can acquire this kind of ability to feel the sensation of other people's movements, then you should gradually both be able to develop an orthodox golf swing and learn to control the mental situation, through a combination of imitation and role-playing.

Many of the keys to improving golf depend very largely on being able to control the mental situation. Most golfers fully appreciate that their own loss of ability in certain circumstances is because of some detrimental thoughts that are entering the mind. Golfers all too readily admit that they were either distracted by someone watching or put off by the overall conditions under which they were playing. Having perfect mental control in this way is undoubtedly a question of practice and exercise. Try to be able to reproduce any specific situation you want. Imagine that you are winning in a match when in fact you are losing. Imagine that you are playing from a specific tee when in fact you are playing from another tee. Learn to use your imagination to create the desired mental state and to control the game as you desire.

> **Spend a few minutes each day imagining the golfing experience in all the senses. Try to visualize the swing and habits of a world-class golfer, retaining an image of the swing and trying to 'feel' yourself performing these movements.**

The invisible target

The shotmaking aspect of the game has one substantial, inherent problem for the golfing mind. Golf is one of the few sports where the ultimate target is rarely in the field of vision as the ball is struck. Other sportsmen face such difficulty only in exceptional situations; the golfer has the problem for every shot but the shortest putt. This requires the player to develop a tremendous mental awareness of the target, enabling him to look physically at the ball through impact and yet to hold an equally vivid picture of the target in the mind. Without this image, the player's shotmaking ability is reduced either by a tendency to look up prematurely at the target or by pure lack of target orientation and directional control.

6 Relaxation and Concentration: The Dangers of Trying Too Hard

Good advice for any golfer who is about to embark on playing in some form of tournament or other is to relax and enjoy it. Perhaps the worst thing that can happen to any golfer is to become tense. Physical tension produces a change in the working of the muscles and with it an alteration in technique; mental tension usually results in loss of concentration and with it a wandering of the imagination. The essence of playing really good golf in any potentially tense situation is to relax both physically and mentally.

Most golfers suffer in competition by simply trying too hard. Obviously there are those who are born competitors and who do well at any game through an ability to perform well under pressure, responding positively to the extra adrenaline that may be produced. Some competitors thrive on pressure and can only perform well if keyed up. These players are, however, very rare. The vast majority of golfers tend to fall apart under pressure and then perform at far less than their true ability. This is not only the case with club golfers; it is also very largely the case with many professionals of world-class ability. In order to do your best in competition it is first of all necessary to ascertain just what kind of character you are! If you are the very rare kind of player who performs at his best when under tension, then this section is not for you. But don't kid yourself that you thrive on tension and being charged up if in reality you are likely to crumple up when success is within your grasp.

Key-up or low key

Players vary considerably in the way they react to pressure and the strain of a competitive situation. In order to perform well under tournament conditions, particularly at top-class championship level, it is essential for the player to realize what kind of animal he happens to be. It is essential to recognize the kind of arousal level at which you yourself perform best. In training golfers to play well during competitions, whether at club or national championship level, it is important for the coach to realize what makes the player 'tick'. In some sports it is essential for players to perform at a very high arousal level; mind and body are keyed-up for performance and adrenaline flows readily and helps boost performance. Particularly in sports where speed and tremendous physical effort are required, the top-class performer may have to go through a process of charging himself up both mentally and physically in order to produce a peak performance.

In the relatively slow, contemplative sports where total concentration may be required for several hours, many players need to dampen their arousal level. They need to make a conscious effort *not* to get charged up and thereby overreact, losing the exactness of technique involved. Golfers who become too charged up under tournament conditions may begin to feel too jerky and jumpy to control the short game adequately, too tense and nervous to swing

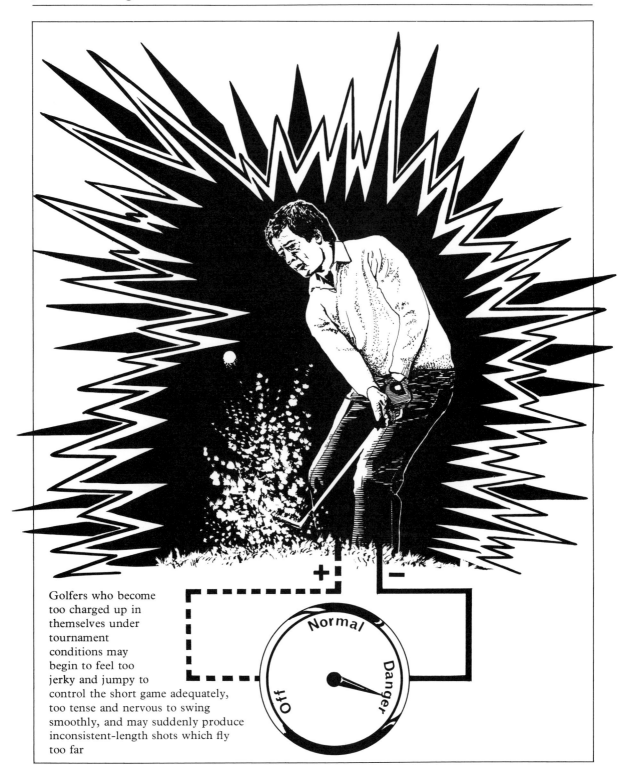

Golfers who become too charged up in themselves under tournament conditions may begin to feel too jerky and jumpy to control the short game adequately, too tense and nervous to swing smoothly, and may suddenly produce inconsistent-length shots which fly too far

smoothly, and may suddenly produce inconsistent-length shots which fly too far. It is a question of realizing how stress and pressure affect you individually and whether you perform better when keyed-up or when relaxed.

The coach not only needs to know how his pupils perform physically; he has to be able to understand mental performance and assess the optimum arousal level for each player. Do you perform best if you tell yourself you couldn't really care less, it's only a game, it doesn't really matter what happens and by this time next week you'll have forgotten all about it anyway? Or are you the sort of person who needs to tell yourself on every putt that the whole world depends on it? Do you need to treat every shot as though it is the most important thing in life at that moment? Do you need to pretend every six-foot putt is for the Open Championship?

Controlling arousal level

Having worked out your own reactions, you need to be able to control your own arousal level. Championship performers who find either that they can't eat before a tournament or that they produce excess adrenaline need to go through the process of mentally repeating the type of golfing circumstances on which they thrive. They need to be able to create the right illusion to keep the arousal level spot on. One can certainly look at many championship golfers and have a very good idea of the players' personalities and the type of situation on which each individual thrives. One can look at Arnold Palmer or Gary Player, Tony Jacklin or Seve Ballesteros, and be very certain that they thrive on being tremendously charged up, pumping adrenaline fast and furiously. On the other hand, Ben Hogan or Hale Irwin, Neil Coles or David Graham all give the appearance of thriving on staying super-cool and adopting a very low-key, mechanistic approach to the game.

In playing competitive golf it is therefore important for everything around you to help in producing the keyed-up or low-key state you require. You need a fourball or foursome partner who understands you and reacts in the same way. It is no good having him shouting,

'Come on, let's go! We can do it; we'll show them!', if you personally thrive on a totally couldn't-care-less attitude. Similarly, if you have someone caddying for you he needs to be

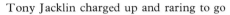

Tony Jacklin charged up and raring to go

tuned in to your wavelength. If you need every possible scrap of enthusiasm and adrenaline to perform well you don't need a disinterested caddy trailing along behind you like the chief mourner. Team captains too can be a godsend or a menace. The rousing, cheering, bullying team captain *may* inspire a super performance in one player and totally destroy another player's attempt at pretending the whole thing is a bundle of fun and doesn't really matter. It takes a very skilled team captain or team coach to be able to enthuse and bully where necessary and yet coax and comfort another player and accept his superficial 'I'm not trying' attitude.

Once you have assessed the level at which you personally perform best, you will have to do

Hale Irwin – supercool with a very controlled approach to the game

everything you possibly can to create the appropriate illusion. Do you thrive on arriving at the last moment, speeding into the car park at seventy miles an hour with a positive, aggressive, charged-up attitude, or do you arrive an hour early and snooze in the corner pretending the whole thing's a dreadful bore? Whichever it is, this is all part of your golf game and a means of creating the optimum mental performance level. Your whole approach to the game and your mental rehearsal of the situation need to focus on achieving the correct arousal level.

Trying too hard

From raw beginner to professional player, many golfers suffer from a tendency towards *trying too hard* when it matters – the fourth of the problems for the golfing mind. *Most players ruin their own golf by trying to force results and trying to make good shots happen.* They keep telling themselves, either mentally or even out loud, that they *must* do such and such a thing or *must* play a certain shot perfectly. This form of mental instruction usually acts only to intimidate. It brings out all the unwanted inhibitions and creates tension. It puts the player under pressure. As soon as any form of mental stress comes into play, the shot that results will usually be a disaster. For this reason the majority of golfers find that they perform worst when they are trying to compel themselves to produce their very best. The player who faces a drive out over a lake, for example, will often ruin his chances of getting over the lake by urging himself to succeed. He tightens up, suffering from self-inflicted pressure, instead of loosening up and allowing himself to swing freely.

In order to play to the best of your ability the mind must stay relaxed, simply adopting an attitude of *allowing* the shots to take place. Playing good golf is a question of freeing your mind and freeing your body, simply allowing the good swing and the correct shots to take place. Don't try to make it happen; *allow* it to happen.

Many golfers ruin their game by trying too hard. They keep telling themselves that they *must* do this or *must* do that. This brings out all the unwanted inhibitions and creates tension, often resulting in a push or slice

Swing – don't steer

A useful pictorial concept is to visualize the ball as being on an enormous piece of elastic, which is attached to your desired landing zone. Simply imagine that all you have to do is to let rip and allow yourself to swing fully and freely so that the ball is released and zooms away through the air to your target at the other end of the elastic. Now the secret of this is that you see the ball as being *released* to do what it wants to do rather than being in any way *made* to do what you want. Try to imagine that the ball is sitting there longing to fly to its target, and that all you have to do is to release it.

More shots at golf are ruined by the player trying to steer the ball in the right direction than by a player who stands up, gives himself freedom and takes a good old whirl at the ball. There is no way that you can actually steer a ball in the right direction. Any attempt to do this simply produces a short, prodding swing, which neither generates any clubhead speed nor squares the clubface up at the right moment. By contrast, a full, free swing, with the hands whooshing away during impact, gives a shot every chance of perfect direction and maximum length. Remember that the ball *wants* to go on target and all you have to do is to release it.

The constant effort concept

Many golfers will not understand what trying too hard means. They will frequently say, 'Yes, but you have to try to play your best and try as hard as you can in a competition.' This is the wrong kind of attitude. The correct way to think about playing golf is to treat each single shot you play as a separate little task you want to perform to the best of your ability. You should obliterate from your mind any shots that have gone before, whether earlier in the round or the day before or last week or whenever. You should relentlessly try to play *every* shot as well as you can. After all, if you are playing a 5 iron to a green, your objective is presumably to put the ball straight down the hole. And you should be aiming to do this every time you play the shot. Your thoughts on this should be exactly the same whether you are practising, playing a few holes in the evening while walking the dog, or playing in the final of your most important tournament. In order to become a good golfer you have to train yourself to approach each of these shots in exactly the same way. The task, after all, is always the same: to get the ball from A to B. If you are trying to hit the ball to a target on every shot, you cannot suddenly improve your results by trying any harder. The level of

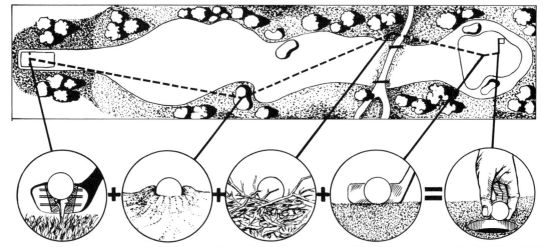

The correct way to think about golf is to try to treat every single shot you play in an identical manner. Try to obliterate from your mind any shots which have gone before. Each one should be treated as a separate little task which you want to perform to the best of your ability

Learn to swing; don't steer.
Imagine the ball on a huge
piece of elastic attached to
your landing zone. All you
have to do is to swing freely,
let rip and the ball will be
released to fly to the target

effort must remain constant.

You will find that top-class players have a certain pride in performance: they want to do their best with every single shot they hit. You would, for example, find that Jack Nicklaus has the desire to create perfection in each shot in exactly the same way, whether playing a few leisurely holes with his friends or performing in a major championship. Because of his pride in his own performance, he will want to do well on every shot he hits. Club golfers, by contrast, will very often hit a great many shots in a relatively relaxed frame of mind and then make a conscious effort to try harder when they feel the shots really matter. Their level of effort from one shot to the next tends to fluctuate quite markedly and their performance alters accordingly. The club golfer will usually make a particular effort when he wants to do his best, either because the shot facing him is particularly difficult or because he has reached a crucial point in the game. What tends to happen in trying harder than usual is that additional mental pressure is created, resulting in a tightening of the important muscles which are the key to the correct golf swing.

> **Mental tension is often caused by trying too hard on certain shots – creating pressure which the player cannot cope with. To combat this try to treat each shot as a separate little task, creating the ability to treat each with a constant degree of effort.**

So how do you find this elusive ability to stay mentally relaxed? The first and probably the most essential key to mental relaxation is the above-mentioned ability to treat every shot identically as a single, isolated unit.

The thought in your mind on hitting *every* golf shot should be 'I am trying to hit the ball from here to that flag. I want to produce the most perfect golf swing I can and I want the ball to go on target.' You shouldn't ease up on some shots and try particularly hard on others. What

you should not be thinking is 'Help, help. I am six down and not playing very well and the odds are I am going to slice the ball into the bushes just like I did here yesterday.' That is the first improvement; think of each shot as a separate unit and obliterate everything else from the mind. Train yourself to produce a constant level of effort.

The second key to mental relaxation for the majority of golfers is to play in a big match with the idea that it is really just another game; the whole world does not depend upon it. After all, it is only a game. Again this is helping you to pitch your desire and effort at a constant level and to keep your body functioning uniformly.

Don't over-criticize

The third aid to mental relaxation is to avoid being over-critical with yourself. Players frequently go out on a golf course expecting perfection, criticize every shot to themselves and then become convinced they will play badly. What you should try to do when playing a round of golf is to concentrate very hard on every shot but as soon as the ball has left the clubhead develop the ability to ignore its result and simply get on with the next shot. If you are not driving particularly well, for example, do not criticize yourself for a bad drive and walk all the way from the tee to where it landed telling yourself off for being such an idiot. By all means have a couple of practice swings if you think this will help to rectify any fault of technique. But otherwise try to eradicate the shot from your mind immediately the ball has come to rest. Turn your attention to the next task and to mustering up concentration for it.

Self-criticism after every shot does absolutely nothing but destroy your own ego. Try never to criticize any shot as you hit it but purely analyse it objectively and constructively to iron out any further such error. If you can treat every shot in a very detached way without allowing yourself to become self-critical, your confidence tends to run at a much higher level all through your game of golf. Once you become self-critical and start saying things to yourself like 'You must hit

Learn not to be over-critical. Try to
eradicate bad shots from the mind as soon as
they have happened. Turn your attention to
the next task and to mustering up
confidence and concentration for the next
shot: keep your confidence running as high
as possible. Criticize after the round but not
during it

it straight', 'Don't be such an idiot', or 'What's the matter with you today?' you are simply putting yourself under pressure. By all means if you play a great shot give yourself some praise, but just ignore everything else that happens.

Certainly go over your game in your mind once you have finished the round and tear yourself to pieces if you like. But while you are actually on the golf course largely ignore what is happening to the ball and simply think of the shot facing you. If you get out of position on the course, do not keep criticizing yourself for being the silly person who got the ball into trouble. Learn to concentrate purely on the present time.

In order to bring out your best golf in competition, first try to play down the importance of any match; second, treat every shot as a separate little unit to be approached in the same way in every game you play; and, third, remember that self-criticism has its place on the practice ground and after you've come in from the golf course but never when you are actually taking part in competition.

Self-criticism on the golf course is nothing but destructive. Forget each shot as soon as you have hit it and leave self-criticism until the round is over.

Physical relaxation

Golf requires the ability to relax physically. Most club golfers tend to fade or slice the ball and this is almost always a sign of tension creeping into the swing. The more relaxed you can be, the more chance you have, as a rule, of hitting the ball straight. Certain shots require a definite punching type of attack and in these the actions may need a considerable degree of stiffness and firmness. But for the majority of long shots relaxation, particularly in the arms and wrists, is a great boon for most club golfers.

Above: Hubert Green showing the relaxation in the arms and wrists necessary for a free swing and maximum speed and distance

Facing page: Jack Nicklaus relaxing for a few minutes before teeing off in the Open

Many professional golfers are hampered by a tendency to hook or draw the ball, resulting in their hitting the ball vast distances but being perhaps a few yards off line. In some instances they may have to tighten up the swing and create greater firmness in order to control the direction and combat the tendency to hook. But for the majority of golfers the problem is quite the opposite. Theirs is a tendency to slice or fade with insufficient freedom and distance. Usually, either they are hampered in swinging through the ball by allowing tension to creep into the arms and wrists, or their leg work is inhibited and the movements insufficiently free. Relaxation in the limbs is one of the great keys to playing better golf.

Tension takes on a number of forms. The beginner who becomes tense and holds his breath will often lift his whole rib cage and produce topped shots. The club golfer who tightens his leg and arm muscles in an attempt to exert power will often inhibit clubhead speed. Beginner, club player and professional alike who tighten up in the hands and wrists will usually fail to square the swing and clubface up in impact producing shots which are blocked away to the right. Tension is a problem for us all.

It is essential in playing good golf, particularly with the long clubs, to stay relaxed at address. Hitting the ball a long way is a question of generating clubhead speed – not force in the body – and hitting the ball straight is very largely a question of utilizing a sound grip by producing freedom in the arms and wrists. It is all too easy for players to get tense right from the moment of address. Many players don't realize that this happens; others appreciate that they become tight in their set up but seem unable to combat it. This added degree of tension is often the key to a difference in performance on the practice ground from the golf course. The set up and whole approach to the game is likely to be far more relaxed on the driving range or practice ground than it is in a playing situation. Add to this the burden of playing in a competition and tension can creep in to such a degree that the swing disintegrates.

In looking at any player at address the key to relaxation very often lies in the shoulders. There are two distinct ways as far as the shoulders are concerned that one can stand to the golf ball. In the correct, and far more relaxed, position the feeling should be one of standing up with the shoulders relaxed downwards and the arms literally hanging down to take hold of the club. The shoulders will feel to be literally pushed downwards and both arms hang relatively close to the side. If one adopts this position and looks in a mirror, the area around the collarbone appears nice and relaxed. There should be no sign of tension in the neck, and the shoulders can be pushed down and the arms can hang freely. Top-class golfers are often unaware of the subtle change in the address position which can so easily occur once tension takes its toll. The key then to maintaining a good, relaxed position at address is to have a couple of deep breaths with the further routine of forcing the shoulders down and back and letting the arms hang loose to the side before adopting the address position under pressure.

In order to be relaxed on the golf course it is necessary to be able to relax in non-golfing situations, to develop this ability to relax at will and then to learn to take it out on to the golf course with you. Many people find it difficult to relax. Their bodies are usually tense, and this can often be seen by raised shoulders and tight-looking hands as well as in the expressions of the face. Spending ten minutes morning and afternoon or evening in total relaxation helps restore both mental and physical energy. Try to develop this ability to be able to cast aside the tensions of the day by sitting for five or ten minutes in a totally relaxed position, allowing all the tension to drain out of the body and new energy to enter.

Relaxation exercises

Sit in a chair and first of all allow your shoulders to drop, breathing deeply and concentrating on your own breathing. Now start with your toes and first of all clench them so that you feel them gripping hard beneath your feet. Now release your toes and feel your whole foot gradually relaxing. Tighten up the arch of the foot and then again allow it to relax. Work systematically right up through your feet and your legs and gradually through to your arms and your hands, clenching your fingers in the same way and then throwing them out into a relaxed position. Gradually you should find that you can adopt a relaxed position relatively quickly and easily.

An excellent way of relaxing both physically and mentally is to sit in a comfortable chair, eyes closed, imagining the room gradually filling with soft, pink air. Imagine this seeping upwards into the room so that with every breath you take you inhale the air so that it circulates through your whole body. The colour pink is important; it is a relaxing, warm kind of colour which tends to bring on a subdued, relaxed state of mind.

Having developed the ability to relax away from the golf course, obviously you must then be able to do exactly the same thing in a golfing context to combat tension. A few deep breaths act as an ideal starting point for physical relaxation; concentrate on your own breathing pattern for mental relaxation. Try then to lower your shoulders, hang your arms and fingers loosely downwards and try to imagine that tension actually drips out of the end of your fingers so that they become totally free and floppy. You may find it helps to go so far as to imagine 'drops of tension' dripping out of your fingers and on to the ground; if you do this your mind may well be taken off the situation causing the tension. If you adopt the correct type of relaxation you will probably feel that the tips of your fingers become warm and fleshy, soft and sensitive. Try also to feel that your wrists in particular are extremely loose before setting up to attack the golf ball. Shake your hands and wrists to get them as loose and free as you can, releasing all possible tension.

Clubhead speed

For those golfers who find that tension creeps into their game, it is important to realize what happens when the golf ball is struck and how maximum distance is produced. Clubhead speed is generated largely with the wrists. The left arm is certainly the guiding force in the

backswing and in the change of direction at the top of the swing. But in the hitting zone the right hand has to generate as much power as it can, and in the full, flowing swing the left arm has to get out of the way in order to allow the right one to work fully. Speed is generated in the impact zone by the right hand producing a kind of throwing action. This action is very similar to the sort of action you would use in throwing a ball overarm. If you imagine yourself throwing a ball you will see that your right wrist, assuming you are right-handed, is perfectly relaxed and gives a tremendous flicking type of action – a very sudden movement – as the ball is released.

The same thing has to happen as you *release* in the hitting zone with a golf club. The left arm has to fold out of the way – again the problem of the two-handed game – in the correct manner to enable the release to take place. The mistake many golfers make in assessing a top-class player at impact is to look at still photographs of this part of the swing, to see that the left arm is straight just beyond impact and to assume that the left arm is therefore stiff. The left arm is straight, not because it is braced in a stiff position, but rather because it is swinging at speed and is therefore flung out through the ball. Beyond impact the left arm has to be able to fold neatly into the body in order to get out of the way and allow the right arm to travel on through in an uninhibited manner. Working with the two arms and hands in conjunction in the golf swing often causes tension and stops the golfer from generating speed. If the left arm does get in the way of the right or if tension is created in the right wrist, this throwing action is inhibited. The action would then be much more like the action of a shot-put in athletics. In other words it becomes a tense, pushing movement rather than a free, throwing movement. Relaxation is absolutely essential in order to generate maximum speed and produce optimum distance.

The player who can relax his arms and wrists will usually also hit the ball straight or may in fact produce a slight draw to shots. Although the top professional golfer is usually satisfied with his own distance, hits the ball a considerable way and may if anything need to tighten up his swing in order to work at exceptional accuracy, even he may have to work at looseness and relaxation under the pressure of a championship. Any player whose hands and wrists become tense and rigid almost certainly fails to produce the correct throwing action through impact, leaving the clubface open with a ball fading away to the right. A bad shot of this kind is a continual occurrence for many club golfers; it is also the telltale sign of momentary tension and weakness under pressure for the professional player.

Developing the ability to relax and countering tension is an important asset. Again it is a question of repetition. If you can adopt a routine of sitting and relaxing for ten minutes a day, casting aside all forms of tension, you should soon be able to take this type of feeling out on to the golf course with you. It is a question of recognizing when tension is creeping into your mind and your body and then immediately taking a few deep breaths, concentrating on your breathing pattern and then systematically dispelling all forms of tension, whether physical or mental.

> **Physical tension as a rule inhibits the arms and wrists through impact, producing a 'blocked' shot to the right – the telltale sign of pressure.**

Facing page: Mark James showing the way in which the left arm must fold away beyond impact to enable the clubhead to travel at full speed

Below: Isao Aoki, an unorthodox swing, but demonstrating the relaxation needed in the arms and wrists for generating clubhead speed. An excellent example for the club player

Quieting the mind and concentration

Although a round of golf can take anywhere between three and five hours to play, the actual time one spends concentrating on shots is relatively short. The golfer who plays reasonably quickly may well spend only about twenty or thirty seconds on planning and executing each shot, but during this brief period his mind needs to be absolutely concentrated. Any susceptibility to outside distractions is likely to cause the odd disaster. Some championship golfers – Ben Hogan, for example – achieve this tremendous concentration by wrapping themselves in a cocoon of thought for the entire round of golf, remaining throughout totally absorbed in their own game; they do their utmost to ward off any exterior distractions and

Facing page: Lee Trevino who spends virtually the whole round talking and wisecracking and yet still pinpoints his mind perfectly on each shot

Many players try to concentrate continually from start to finish of the round without a moment's relaxation. This is often too great a strain and results in a deterioration in performance after a couple of hours – around the 12th. Instead, they would be far better to relax more between shots and concentrate only when faced with each specific shot

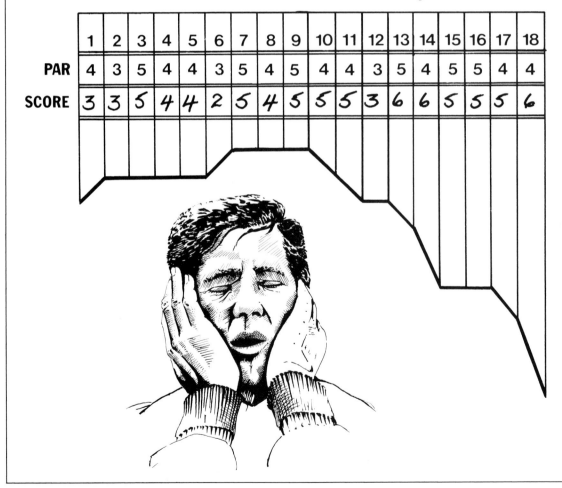

	1	2	3	4	5	6	7	8	9	10	11	12	13	14	15	16	17	18
PAR	4	3	5	4	4	3	5	4	5	4	4	3	5	4	5	5	4	4
SCORE	3	3	5	4	4	2	5	4	5	5	5	3	6	6	5	5	5	6

are usually either unable or unwilling to talk to anybody for fear of being sidetracked. At the opposite end of the spectrum is a player such as Lee Trevino, who spends virtually the whole round talking and wisecracking and yet still pinpoints his mind perfectly on each shot.

Many golfers who find difficulty in concentrating try to adopt the first kind of approach – continuous concentration throughout the round. They might well do better to adopt the second. *Most people who try to concentrate wholeheartedly for the entire round of golf – without relaxing between shots – are usually mentally unable to concentrate fully for that period of time.* Their concentration usually breaks down after a couple of hours, and this, combined with the mental strain of trying to concentrate, usually leads to a deterioration in performance somewhere around the twelfth hole. By contrast, the person who is relatively relaxed about his game, with a great ability to switch on and off from tremendously pinpointed concentration, will usually be able to keep up this pattern throughout the whole round.

Developing concentration

Learning to fix one's concentration at a 100 per cent level is a question of practice. Most people's minds wander from one thing to another. Try, for example, just sitting in a chair, in a relaxed state, and trying to concentrate on one particular object in the room. You will almost certainly find your mind wandering after a short time. If you don't immediately bring yourself back to the object in question, your thoughts will wander off from one subject to another linked subject and yet another. Eventually you may find yourself thinking about something so remote from your original target of concentration that it is quite difficult in retrospect to see how your process of thought has hopped from one object to the next.

The kind of concentration one needs for golf – unless you set out to be a cocoon-type player – is to have short bursts of less than a minute's deep, unwavering concentration which resists all possible outside distraction. As an exercise, start by taking an object which is some kind of

container – a box, an ashtray, a cup – something with an inside and an outside. Place this in front of you on a table and then focus your attention on the object and try to concentrate on it so fiercely that you become entirely oblivious of everything else surrounding it. First choose one particular point on the outside of the container and concentrate on that, without allowing any other thought to enter your mind except the object itself. Try to do this for as long as you can. Gradually move your thoughts right round the outside of the container until you begin to be able to think of it from all other angles. Then move your concentration to the inside of the container so that you begin to focus on it as though from inside. As soon as you find yourself being distracted and thinking of anything else whatsoever, take yourself back to the front of the object and then again work your way right round the outside, over and into the inside. You will gradually find not only that you can cut out all other forms of visual distraction but that you can, with practice, cut out auditory distraction. By practising in this way you should find that your span of concentration gradually lengthens until you are able to focus your attention for relatively long periods of time without in any way becoming sidetracked.

You must also be able to develop the ability to move from an entirely relaxed mental state, where your thoughts are allowed to wander and your mind is free, to a state of total concentration at a moment's notice. This again is a question of practice and developing a certain technique. The exercise again is one that can be done at home. Choose some specific object which is always to hand. If you are a keen golfer and there is nothing particularly unusual in your having the odd golf ball sitting around – as invariably happens in my home – use a golf ball as your target object. If not, select something else. Practise switching your concentration periodically from whatever else you were doing to your chosen object. Stop watching the television during advertisements, for example, and try to focus your attention so thoroughly on the object that you begin to be able to cut out all outside visual and auditory distractions. With repeated exercise the mind soon develops great

It is necessary to be able to produce immense concentration for each particular shot, using a couple of key thoughts to focus the mind and to shut out all extraneous distractions. Take a couple of deep breaths, focus on ball and target and adopt a pair of mental blinkers to pinpoint your attention

powers of concentration and can be made so selective in its focusing and attention that awareness of the object in question becomes exceptionally bright, while the background can be made to fade away into oblivion.

Such is the kind of concentration one requires on the golf course. The golfer who wants to perform at his best needs to be able to produce this intense concentration at will for each particular shot, casting out all unnecessary thoughts and distractions and instead having total awareness of the task in hand. In order to bring about this state on the golf course the player should develop one or two key thoughts which bring his mind back from the general to the specific. Before facing every shot, after you have taken two or three deep breaths, focused your attention on the pattern of your breathing and forced tension to drip from your fingertips, move your attention on to the ball and target and in turn to the shot facing you.

The process of concentration requires you to assess the shot you want to produce and to choose the club. From there you must pinpoint your attention on the target, mentally rehearsing the movements to follow until you have a perfect feeling of the desired swing, the strike you want to produce and in turn the flight of the ball. During this process of intense concentration just before the shot, you must expel all outside thoughts, quickly establishing yourself in your own little world with a mental 'high' for a span of perhaps a minute. It is rather like looking through the viewfinder of a camera: you are focusing only on the target, and all extraneous sights (and sounds) fade into oblivion. You are left with nothing but an awareness of the clubhead, ball and target and a positive desire to produce the shot you want. Golfers and other sportsmen who acquire this exceptional mental concentration frequently find that their super-awareness during performance is accompanied by an extraordinary clarity of mind and a sensation of time slowing down. Tremendous concentration may indeed lead to a semi-hypnotic state in which awareness of the environment fades, while the body and mind achieve quite exceptional levels of performance with the task in hand.

Psychokinesis: mind over matter

This self-hypnotic state of exceptional concentration for the championship-level performer may almost lead to the sensation of mind and body existing separately – the mind taking on powers of its own outside normal experience.

Whether or not one is prepared to accept that there is some form of sixth sense, the evidence of researchers in the world of the paranormal at least provides food for thought. Psychokinesis is the effect of mind over matter whereby an inanimate object is literally moved by the forces of the mind. You may, of course, simply reject any such concept, either through fear of the unknown or through an inherent resistance to changing your views.

Demonstrations of possible mental control over inanimate objects are not particularly new, but in recent years there have been exhaustive attempts at investigating claims of paranormal powers under rigorous experimental conditions. Occasionally such claims have been accepted as hoaxes, while on other occasions the experimenters have had to admit that there appears to be some force of mind which can indeed generate external power. Such power may take the form of thought transference or may produce a force that is able to move an inanimate object. Russian experiments, in particular, have enabled researchers to photograph a field of force around a living object in very much the same way as one might plot a magnetic force around a metallic object. Medical researchers suggest that sheer willpower can cure cancer if the patient turns the forces of the mind towards the tumour and concentrates on its destruction.

Although, if put as a direct question, most readers would almost certainly reject the claims to truth of psychokinesis, most would also accept that certain golfers do indeed appear to 'will' the ball to do what they want – and usually with successful results. One can almost feel the force Gary Player generates by trying to will the

Gary Player 'willing' the ball on its way

ball into the hole. Spectators can sense the mental electricity generated by Arnold Palmer or Seve Ballesteros, as they extricate themselves from no-man's-land. And certainly you cannot help but be aware of Jack Nicklaus's piercing stare as he holes an enormous putt or thunders a drive down the fairway. Their fellow competitors frequently suggest – whether seriously or semi-seriously – that such players perform with the assistance of some extra mental power.

One may glibly talk of willing the ball into the hole or of mind over matter. But just how beneficial can acceptance of such a mental force be to the aspiring golfer? It is, of course, true that the force a golfer generates from his mind may act in one or other of two ways. By sheer concentration and an unerring belief that the ball is going to react in response to tremendous desire, the body may in fact be programmed into performing the task perfectly. In other words, it is the excessive concentration that is mustered up which produces perfection. On the other hand, one may fully accept that this enormous concentration of the mind's resources on the golf ball does actually produce a controlling physical force. Perhaps it is a combination of both. Certainly a belief in an internal power to influence the golf ball would be an asset. Sporting folklore is full of stories of success assisted through the powers of the mind: players who have overcome pain and injury while performing through a focusing of the mind; vast crowds who believe they can will their team to success; legendary footballers like Pelé who, many contemporaries claim, could even make an oncoming ball swerve in mid-air.

Undoubtedly, if you can provide yourself with sufficient supporting evidence to create a belief in the phenomenon it can only enhance performance. Belief and concentration themselves are half the battle, at least producing superb control in yourself, even if not in the ball.

If you are able to demonstrate to your own satisfaction that the mind can produce an external force, it will almost certainly lead you to a greater belief in yourself. With this belief you may well feel a greater control of the ball and a greater confidence in your own overall ability. If you are prepared to take the risk of sitting for an hour, perfectly still and quiet, focusing your whole attention on some small, light object, with an intense desire to move it, but nothing happens, you have lost nothing. You may be left with some doubt whether your attention was sufficiently concentrated or whether your mind was allowed to wander. If you can in fact find such perfect, controlled concentration – without the bonus of creating movement in something inanimate – then this achievement in itself will enhance your mental resources. For the championship golfer the rewards can be enormous, attuning oneself to the sensation of the semi-hypnotic state of perfect concentration. For those of lower aspiration the rewards of sensing a totally concentrated experience will make the experiment worthwhile. If a movement can be produced purely from mental force, the effect on your golf and self-belief may be dramatic. Even if no such movement occurs, the intense concentration will almost certainly produce a changed mental state and possibly a feeling of immense power and control.

7 Judgements and the Stationary Ball

Striking a stationary ball creates certain mental problems. The only physical problem with regard to the stationary ball in golf is that the ground tends to get in the way of the beginner's swing. The mental problems arise because playing a stationary ball gives longer to think about the task than when striking a moving ball. All stationary-ball players frequently have un-productive thoughts combined with quite the wrong approach to situation assessment and decision-making. 'The problem of the stationary ball' is at the heart of the scoring stage of playing the game and permits the golfing mind to be at its most destructive.

Speed of judgements

Golf is unlike the majority of ball games where the highly skilled performer works very largely with reflex actions that are essentially spon-taneous responses to the movement of the ball or the shots of another player. The soccer or tennis player, rugby player or cricketer de-velops most of his skills around speedy reac-tions and split-second timing. The thought processes have to be decisive but responsive and reflexive. Throughout the majority of playing time of these sports the fast-moving ball is in the perfect position for striking only for a fraction of a second. Speed is essential and decisions are made rapidly without time for great contem-plation or consideration of the situation.

By contrast, there are other periods in these games where the thinking process takes on a completely different character. The tennis player serving, the cricketer bowling and the rugby player attempting a penalty kick are all faced with a completely different kind of mental task. In these cases the player is totally in control of the timing and makes the decision when to put the ball into play. At this point in the game the thinking process ceases to be a spontaneous response to a moving ball and the player is able to consider quite fully all the factors in the game. This is where the stress of the situation and competitive pressure are all too likely to show. We now have the difficulties caused by 'the problem of the stationary ball'. There is simply too much time for thinking.

The tennis player returning a serve from his opponent has a brief instant in which to reach for the ball and drive it towards his target. If he is concentrating on the game in hand, his mind at the moment the ball hurtles over the net towards him has little room for considering the match situation or his own technique. On the other hand, when he is faced with serving the ball to his opponent there is all too much time for extraneous thoughts to enter the mind and inhibit freedom of performance and thus dampen the natural skill of the player. A movement which is very easy during practice may suddenly become difficult when tension is created through over-analysing the techniques involved and the tournament conditions pre-vailing. One would expect the top-class tennis player to be able to serve a tennis ball faultlessly into the appropriate position in his opponent's court, but this is certainly not always the case. The percentage accuracy in practice may drop dramatically under certain high-pressure tour-nament situations. And yet, of course, the physical task in hand is precisely the same.

What makes the difference is the state of the player's mind.

In just the same way, the rugby player may well find it considerably more difficult to kick a stationary ball through the goalposts when converting a try than he would if the ball were moving. It is almost certainly not the action involved in kicking a stationary ball which is the difficulty but rather that this allows his slower thought processes to play their part. Again his feelings of tension and his inhibitions over success and failure are likely to restrict his natural reflex actions.

Worsened judgement

One of the great difficulties in this part of any sport is that judgement of the situation tends to be worsened. The majority of performers in any sport of this kind build up a very strong pattern of reflex behaviour which allows them to sum up the situation in a fraction of a second, transmitting the situation from the brain to the muscles in such a way that they respond quite naturally to the conditions facing them. The player may take a split-second look at his target and this is instantaneously transmitted to the muscles of the appropriate limb so that the strike of the ball usually carries just the right weight and direction. As soon as the player is faced with a situation where the slow functions of the mind come into play, his judgement tends to be inhibited by a much more deliberate but less accurate process of analysis.

If the player were able to trust his own split-second judgement, built up through years of practice and tournament play, then the action would be free and performance optimum. But as soon as the slower process is allowed to take over, the player frequently tries to force some kind of judgement to take place by willing himself or trying to force himself not to make an error. When he does this his natural judgemental skill tends to be lost through some breakdown in communication and coordination between the visual and mental input and the physical, muscular output. Players in these kinds of sports, where there is a mixture of

reflex movement and considered movement, are at least able to compare performance under the differing thought processes. The top-class performer may readily see the wisdom of reverting to his high-speed, instinctive processes in those parts of the game which permit time for consideration.

> **Playing a stationary ball in many ways gives too much time for thinking. Instead of relying on fast-speed, reflex thinking, the player often adopts a slow-speed form of analysis which is often less accurate.**

Time for thought

On the other hand, there are other sports where the thought processes are slow and considerate and virtually never reflexive and spontaneous – golf, snooker, bowls, rifle shooting and many of the athletic field events such as high jump and javelin throwing. In these sports the great barrier to top-class performance is very often the player's inability to focus sufficiently well on the task in hand; instead he becomes distracted by extraneous thought and over-awareness of the competitive situation that faces him. These sports are therefore in many ways more mentally demanding than the fast-action sports.

The great difficulty for players of these various sports is very often one of producing a top-level performance when it matters and being able to reproduce the kind of results that

The tennis player returning serve relies on split-second timing and spontaneous judgement. In stationary ball games the player determines how long he waits before putting the ball into play. Frequently, the golfer is relaxed and relatively spontaneous in practice, slows down and changes his thought pattern in play, and then becomes even slower and more deliberate under pressure. Far from this added concentration aiding the assessment, it dampens the brain's ability to make high speed, emergency decisions and judgement frequently deteriorates

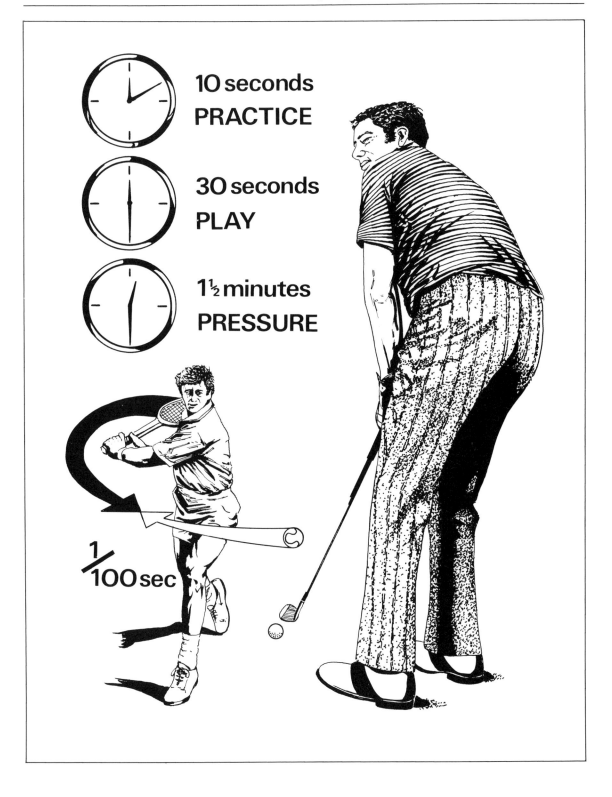

10 seconds PRACTICE

30 seconds PLAY

1½ minutes PRESSURE

1/100 sec

are produced during practice. Of these, golf is perhaps the most demanding because it involves so many different playing situations and such a great variety of shots. While the exponent of the other sports is very largely involved with repeating the same kind of action over and over again, the golfer is continually having to adapt to the length and height of shot as well as the difference in the playing surface and ground contours. In the track events there are easily evaluated performance levels which may separate one athlete from another. But, even in these, the essence of the top-class performer is to be able to produce the right results on the major occasions. In others of these 'thinking' sports the level of physical ability between the various players may be virtually imperceptible. A championship may hinge almost entirely on the ability of players to reproduce the results consistently over a period of several hours. In these types of situations the player is faced with the difficult task of keeping his performance at its optimum level for every shot, and keeping his decision-making and judgemental skills up to scratch.

The slow-speed sport

Golf is perhaps the most interesting of these slow-speed, 'thinking' sports, for the difference between a good shot and a bad shot is particularly noticeable and punishing. Each shot in golf, on any particular hole, is dependent for position upon the shot that has gone before. Thus a bad shot produces a bad situation from which the next shot has to be played. Despite this, the golfer must, if he is to produce a good score, be able to treat each specific shot as a separate unit so that his approach to each shot remains consistent. As soon as the golfer permits himself to think in terms of what has gone before the shot in hand, or if he lets himself think of the dangers of any shot which is to follow, his concentration on the task facing him at that moment tends to be reduced and too many unnecessary thoughts are often likely to cloud the mind.

Perfect awareness and understanding of the two-speed judgement process can considerably change a player's performance. What is usually not appreciated is that many players who perform at a relatively high level of skill begin to play golf in various situations with what equates very largely to the fast-speed, reflex action found in the moving-ball sports. One of the great dangers for many golfers is that they adopt an entirely different thought process from practice to play, or again from relatively unpressured play to tournament-level conditions. Many golfers can be seen on the practice ground or driving range setting up to one ball after another, giving a very brief look at the target, and then sending the ball on its way without a moment's hesitation. The good golfer who does this takes a quick look at the target and this input is transmitted from the brain to the muscles in a split second, giving the body its set of instructions for the required swing. By practising in this way the player is adopting virtually the same form of judgement as the tennis player is able to use, for although the ball is stationary the thought process occurs in such a minute period of time that there is no room for consideration of outside events or emotions.

> **Many golfers rely on reflex thoughts and decision-making in practice but change to the slower, analytical thinking process in play.**

For the majority of golfers there comes a point where their thinking process tends to change from one speed to the other. With players of a lower-level skill or where the technique requires constant adjustment, this change may emerge immediately the player leaves the practice ground and goes on to the golf course, when the player's skill at striking the ball almost always drops quite noticeably. Instead of looking at the target and relying on the form of judgement he would have used on the practice ground, he somehow pressures himself into over-analysing the situation, with the assumption that this is going to improve his performance. Realistically, if he is the kind of player who needs to consider the shot in hand particularly carefully before executing it, then he needs to adopt this kind of approach to every shot hit in practice as well. More commonly, however, his timing and form of concentration during practice probably bring out his maximum potential, whereas analysing the situation too closely may suppress his true level of performance.

The 'tournament' approach

More common, and particularly noticeable among the better-standard performer, is the tendency to alter the thinking process in a tournament or wherever the player is under some kind of pressure to produce his best performance. Frequently the player begins to produce shots which are unrepresentative of his real level of skill. He may therefore find a certain frustration at not being able to produce his best results under the strain of a competition. *What he often fails to realize is that he has changed his whole mental approach to the striking of each ball by changing from a high-speed, natural approach to one of a far slower, more deliberate, analytical nature.* The player, in fact, frequently alters the function of his own thought processes *in the wrong direction* in an attempt to correct the low-level performance which is the cause of the problem. The player may well have experienced a lowering in his standard in a tournament and fallen into the trap of thinking that he needs to concentrate harder or make an even more determined effort to produce his very best results. Very rarely does he appreciate that the answer to the problem lies in moving his thought process back in the other direction so that he allows himself the spontaneity he would have given himself in practice or during relaxed play.

> **The tournament player often sees his failure as one of insufficient thought and concentration. He consciously becomes more analytical on the course instead of moving his thoughts in the other direction and trying to rely on more reflex judgements.**

The golfer who is able to perform at top-class championship level is able to control his mental processes so that he adopts very much the same approach in his practice as he does under the most strenuous tournament conditions. Either this may mean adapting his thinking speed during practice in order to be more deliberate and therefore to match what he does on a golf course, or, more commonly, it will require self-persuasion to allow the natural skill to play its part without excessive analysis.

It is essential for the tournament player to produce a systematic approach to every shot – an exact pattern of preparation which gives no margin for change and, particularly, for slowing down and loss of spontaneity. Ideally, from the moment the club is selected for any shot, the ritual begins – one practice swing, two looks at the target, or whatever. It requires an exactness with every kind of shot, from putting to driving, each with its own specific routine. There should be no extra look at the hole, no fidgeting or fussiness or slowing down in tournaments. Instead the game should be seen as one where fast-speed, reflex thoughts are generally the most productive, and slow-speed analysis at times destructive. Pitch, chip and putt more quickly and spontaneously for perfect judgement. Speed it up; don't slow it down.

Visual input

Because golf is one of the great 'thinking' sports a full awareness of the mental processes involved is just as important to the good golfer as is an awareness of the physical techniques. The player who is aware of the thoughts in his own mind soon appreciates what an immense and finely tuned programme of muscle memory is stored there. When he looks at a specific target or imagines the flight of the ball in a specific way, his muscles respond quite spontaneously to this visual input in order to produce the desired shot.

For many shots in golf, perception of the target produces the visual input that programmes the mind and body to react in a certain way. Transmission of the target, as it were, keys the

golfer into swinging the golf club in precisely the correct manner. There is virtually no other instruction he needs to give himself other than an accurate picture of where he wants the ball to land. In other kinds of golf shots the optimum level of visual input comprises a picture not of the target but instead of *a perfectly traced path of the required flight of the ball*. This visual input needs to be conjured up in the mind, preferably in as real and clear a manner as possible. In just the same way as the picture of the target provides the correct set of instructions for certain kinds of shots, so the imagined flight of the ball sets the body into a programme for producing the visualized flight.

The top-class golfer is very largely dependent upon being able to produce the correct picture in his mind so that this serves as the set of instructions upon which his body works. He therefore needs very perfect control over his imagination. If there is any tendency to permit negative pictures to enter the mind, by repeating to himself 'I don't want to do this', then these particular pictures become the set of instructions which direct his body. All such negative thoughts therefore have to be cleared from the mind and the right ones allowed to take over.

One of the great difficulties encountered by top-class golfers is that their ability to produce the right mental instructions is frequently distorted or inhibited by competitive pressures. If the player finds himself standing prepared for a shot without the correct picture in his mind, trying too hard and making too many laborious judgements about the situation usually results in loss of freedom and performance. Once again, this is often the result of over-analysis and a loss of the high-speed mental process. *As soon as the brain is allowed to switch from fast-level thinking to slow-level thinking, the imaginative functions often fall away or become subdued.* Top-class golf requires the ability not only to make sound judgements and decisions, but to make such judgements in the correct manner at the height of competition.

Doubt and indecision

Capitalizing on your own technique in order to score well depends on understanding the golf course, making sensible decisions about strategy and approach, and learning from your mistakes. Many golfers ruin their chance of scoring well not so much by taking wrong decisions as by being indecisive on the golf course. Any element of doubt over the approach to a shot is likely to result in the player failing to be positive in the way he attacks the ball, producing a halfhearted swing with little chance of success. It is essential in playing every shot to have a positive aim in mind, to be confident over the shot you are playing and the club you have chosen, and to produce a swing that is solid and authoritative. The swing needs to be uninhibited – leaving no room for doubt and indecision to restrict the attack on the ball. *Any swing that is executed while uncertainty and negative thoughts dominate the mind is almost certain to decelerate into the impact zone as the player subconsciously changes course en route to the ball.* The player who is prone to slicing will usually slice; the player who is prone to hooking will usually hook. In fact, doubt and uncertainty almost always bring out the worst in any golf swing.

Whatever decision you take on the golf course, it must be a positive one and it must be firmly made before executing the shot. There is no point whatsoever in hitting a golf shot while you are in any way uncertain about the club you have chosen, the line you are taking or the way in which you are trying to strike the ball. *It is better on the whole to make a wrong but positive decision and at least strike the ball with authority than to produce a swing that is guided by two contrasting thoughts.*

Decision-making

Decision-making on the golf course is largely a question of mental discipline. The first step is to

---

Tom Watson is a great example for all, keeping his timing and rhythm identical from the start of a tournament to the finish, never faltering from his pattern or slowing down under pressure

It is essential to have a positive approach to every shot and never to doubt the club chosen. Any tendency towards indecision usually leads to a slowing down of the swing, for some players causing a hook, for others a slice. In many ways it is better to make a wrong but positive decision and at least strike the ball with authority than to produce a swing guided by contrasting thoughts decide exactly where you are trying to hit the ball. Many golfers fail to choose a definite target on all shots and simply have in mind some kind of general area where they are trying to aim. The target must be exact, even if you are not the calibre of golfer who can expect to position the ball particularly accurately. Players frequently come unstuck at the type of holes that require a definite decision over positioning the ball. The hole may, for example, give you two definite alternatives of playing to the right or to the left of a hazard, perhaps needing different choices of clubbing. It is essential as a first step to choose the exact target you are aiming at, for both direction and distance. If there is any doubt in your mind over where you are aiming, then you are not ready to take the next decision on club selection. Choose a target and be absolutely single-minded about this choice.

Faced with this target, you then have to assess the weather conditions, effective distance for clubbing purposes and the way in which you are trying to play the ball. Are you aiming to the left and allowing the wind to push the ball back on target? Are you aiming at the target and trying to draw it against the wind? Are you going to hit the ball with a standard full shot or are you going to try to punch the ball firmly on target? At this point you have to make a fairly quick decision about your plan of campaign for striking the ball on target.

Many golfers at this point, both amateur and professional, are left with unclear pictures in their mind and no real decision. They so easily get caught between two types of shot and fail to make a proper swing.

Stating your objectives

For the player who finds himself playing shots indecisively, the key solution is to make a verbal statement to yourself of your intentions. Once you tell yourself the object of the swing, it commits you to a certain course of action and usually makes it easier to adhere to that objective. You will often hear good players stating to their caddies or to someone else in earshot exactly what they are intending to do. This isn't a question of conceit; it is rather that the player

realizes that making a definite public statement about what he plans to do gives him the necessary certainty in his own mind and doesn't allow his own mental set of instructions to wander around disastrously. Lee Trevino is a great example of this. You will often hear him announcing exactly what he intends to do with shots – not, as many people think, as a way of saying 'Look, aren't I clever', but rather as a means of getting his own concentration on track and producing a really single-minded approach to a particular shot. The lesson is a good one. If you are in two minds about the way in which you are going to approach the shot, then tell yourself exactly what you are going to do, not relying on vague, muddled thoughts but making a positive verbal statement of the decision you have made. 'I am going to hit that ball exactly over the left-hand corner of that bunker and it will kick ten yards left when it lands.' It commits you; it makes you positive. Having committed yourself verbally, commit yourself with a good, positive image of the intended shot.

> **If you suffer from indecision on the course, make a positive, verbal statement of your intentions and it will commit you to a certain shot, repelling indecision.**

Trusting your club

Choosing the right club also requires a positive decision in exactly the same way. Again it is absolutely no use trying to hit the ball while unsure about the club you have taken. It is essential to trust the club you have chosen and to hit it authoritatively. Club golfers generally can be seen to produce bad shots as soon as there is any doubt over the club they have chosen. If you see a club golfer change his mind with his clubbing, you will usually also see him produce a relatively poor, inhibited swing. The professional golfer usually trains himself to cast out any doubt over the club he has chosen and to hit the ball positively with the club he eventually selects. But even for the professional golfer

there is the occasional shot when indecision over clubbing creeps in and the player produces a swing which shows very clearly the doubt in his mind.

If you choose a 5 iron and should have chosen a 6 iron, slowing down and quitting on the ball is not the answer. It usually results in poor distance and a bad contact. If, on the other hand, you have chosen a 6 iron and needed a 5 iron, then nothing you do in the swing is going to make up for the error in selection. Choose the club, have confidence in it and get on with the swing.

Above: Player and caddy need to work hand in hand to produce positive decisions. Never let yourself be sidetracked by anyone else. Rely on your own judgement and choice and make a definite statement to him of what you intend to do

Facing page: Lee Trevino frequently announces what he intends to do with each shot. This clears the mind, commits you and produces a good, positive approach. If you suffer from indecision make a positive, verbal statement of your intentions

Never let yourself be sidetracked into any form of doubt by a caddy or fourball partner. If the caddy hands you a driver on the tee when you had in fact thought of taking a 3 wood, don't ever be afraid of saying 'no'. Rely on your own judgement and choice and make a definite statement to him of what you intend to do. If you get caught halfway between his idea of hitting a driver and your idea of hitting a 3 wood, you are destined for failure. This is then likely to be compounded by further irritation at your stupidity. It is preferable to have a definite idea of the driving clubs you are going to use. Tell your caddy your intentions of using a driver or otherwise before you go off the first tee, letting him know at that time any holes where you won't necessarily hit the driver. On any tee where there is going to be an element of choice, always tell him this before you get to the tee so that there is no question of his pulling out the wrong club for you. The type of person to avoid having around when you play golf, either as a caddy or as a partner, is the one who stands ooh-ing and ah-ing and wringing his hands, thus displaying his doubt over your choice of clubs. Nothing is more likely to destroy your self-confidence in your choice of clubbing and approach to the shot!

Decision-making must be positive. First you choose the positive target. Second, you make a definite statement about what you are attempting to do and, third, you choose a club and trust it. Create a positive image in your mind and avoid any thoughts of what you are trying to avoid. Better to make a wrong decision than not to make one at all.

Judging distance

Scoring well at golf is largely a question of driving the ball well and then of hitting good second shots into the green. There are two important factors in hitting second shots to set yourself up for birdies. The first, of course, is to hit the ball straight. The second is to hit the ball the right distance. *What is important to remember is that ten yards short or ten yards past the flag is equal to ten yards left or right of the flag.* Although this sounds obvious, the majority of golfers either fail to realize this or, if they do realize it, don't improve accordingly.

The low-handicap golfer who pushes a ball with a long iron ten yards right of the target is likely to be quite disgusted with himself. On the other hand, he is quite likely to leave the shot ten yards short or even twenty yards short and hardly realize his errors. The point is this. If you hit the ball out to the side of the flag the error shows. If you hit the ball short of the flag (or unusually past the flag) the error is usually not apparent. You can kid yourself the shot was perfect. A shot ten yards to the side of the flag will look bad. A straight shot ten yards short will probably look extremely good. And yet there is still a ten-yard error, leaving just the same problems in making the birdie or making the par.

Judging distance well is a key to good golf. For the low-handicap golfer there is usually a ten-yard gap between adjacent irons. Most greens are between twenty and forty yards in length. This means that you can very easily hit the ball on to a green and be one, two or even three clubs short of the flag. I say short, because very few people allow themselves to hit the ball past the flag. Most people do not naturally judge distance anything like as well as they imagine they do. On flat ground with no distance cues of any kind, you will probably find it almost impossible to judge distance accurately. If you go out for a walk on a beach or in the park or out on playing fields, pick out a spot, try to assess the distance in your own mind, and then pace out the distance to see just how accurate you are. Most people can be as much as 30 or 40 yards out over a distance of 160 yards or so.

When you are playing on the golf course you have certain distance cues which help you to assess the distance more accurately. To start with, the flag on each green acts as some sort of cue. Second, you may know the kind of distance involved from past experience and, third, the images of the people in front of you again give you some type of visual cue for making your judgement. But, although most golfers of a relatively low handicap maintain that they can judge distance accurately simply by looking at the flag, the majority are nowhere near as accurate as they imagine. To judge with accuracy a distance of 140 or 150 yards is virtually impossible. Once you get to being six or seven yards out in your assessment you are likely to be one club out in your selection. For this reason, almost all top professionals and the majority of top amateurs prepare for a tournament by pacing distances on the golf course from certain landmarks, using these measurements for assessing their clubbing.

Judging distance is just as difficult, if not more so, than judging speed or time. Yet most of us rely heavily on a speedometer in the car and equally rely on using a wrist-watch. Don't be fooled by thinking that you can judge distance accurately. Almost certainly you can't.

> **Ten yards short of the flag is equal to ten yards wide of the flag. Accurately judging distance is essential and also encourages a more positive approach to striking the ball.**

If you aspire to top-level golf, prepare for any championship by measuring distances and certainly measure the distances on your own golf course so that you can use them or get to know them in assisting your general play. All you need is some fairly obvious landmark on any particular hole. Select a certain bunker or tree, pacing from either the back or front of the bunker or from the tree to the front of the green and to the back of the green or, if you prefer, simply to the middle of the green. This will then give you an accurate distance for making your judgements. If you are going uphill, mentally add ten or twenty yards to the measurement. If you are hitting into the wind, similarly add ten or twenty yards in assessing the clubbing. At first you will almost certainly find that some of the distances disagree with what your eye tells

Being ten yards short or ten yards past a flag is just as much of an error as being ten yards to right or left. It just doesn't look as bad. It is all too easy to kid yourself that a shot is perfect when in reality it is ten or twenty yards short through a thoroughly bad decision over clubbing

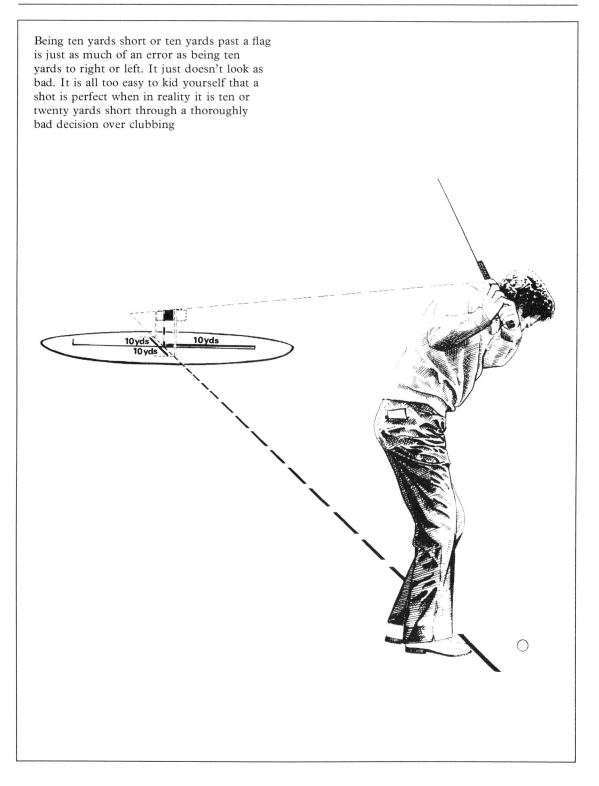

10yds   10yds
10yds

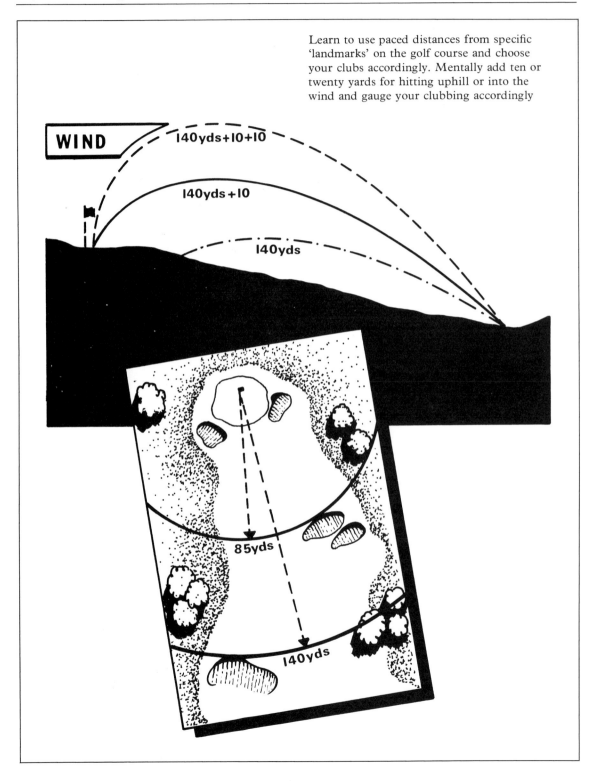

Learn to use paced distances from specific 'landmarks' on the golf course and choose your clubs accordingly. Mentally add ten or twenty yards for hitting uphill or into the wind and gauge your clubbing accordingly

15 yds

15 yds

180 yds

To help you attack the flag, it is helpful to know the distances to the centre of the green and also to any problem area behind the green. In this way you can say to yourself, 'I've got 180 yards to the flag, 195 to the back of the green, and 210 yards before I hit trouble.' You can then be far more positive in choosing the longer of two clubs, knowing your selection is perfectly safe

you. You will undoubtedly find yourself looking at a certain shot and not believing the figure you have in front of you. Although it may take quite a time to learn to trust the yardage, you have to rely heavily on it. Trust the distance and you will soon find that you hit the ball far more confidently, certain that you have the right club and can afford to hit it authoritatively.

The general fault is in failing to take enough club for shots to the green. There are several reasons for this. First, there is the sheer conceit you may have of wanting to hit the green with less club than you really can. Second, you are quite likely to find that you practise at tournaments or play your usual friendly golf with the flag positioned in the middle or at the front of the green. In tournament golf the flags are frequently placed at the back of the green. Accordingly it is often difficult to make yourself hit right to the back. Third, you probably feel progressively more at ease with each shorter club you choose. Another reason, however, is one of visual distortion. If the flag is perhaps two thirds of the way back on the green you may find it difficult to take sufficient club – either because it is not apparent how far back the flag is or because the flag seems so dangerously near the back that it is hard to be sufficiently bold. Do realize that the length of the green tends to be extremely foreshortened, leading to considerable difficulties in judging the true position of the flag.

Clubbing and confidence

Again, if you measure the distances and know the length of the green, you have far more chance of judging where the flag really is, allowing yourself to hit fully at the flag with the confidence that you aren't going to go right through. For the player who is serious about playing good tournament golf, it is well worth measuring the length of the greens. You can then always tell yourself not only what distance you have to the flag but what distance you have to the back of the green and to any trouble beyond it. In this way you can be confident of taking enough club while knowing that you

can't reach the trouble behind the green with a perfect shot.

It is important to keep in mind all the time that when you are hitting into most greens the usual trouble is a bunker short and to the right of the flag and probably also one short and to the left. If you can convince yourself to hit enough club so that you really do try to pitch the ball right at the flag you will usually miss these two bunkers. The player who hits the ball the correct distance into the green will usually avoid most of the greenside bunkers and is quite likely to be less penalized for a slightly off-line shot. Try going out and keeping a record for a few weeks of how often you come up short of the flag compared with how often you go past the flag. Most golfers will go through a green under normal playing conditions only on very rare occasions. It is unusual for the club golfer to pitch the ball right to the back of the green; it is all too common to finish up short by underclubbing. Certainly the best rule when playing a course you don't know at all well is to try to make every single shot you hit, whether iron shot or pitch or chip, go past the flag: difficult to do, but it may revolutionize your scoring.

> **In normal playing conditions try to make every shot you play pass the flag and you may find it revolutionizes your scoring.**

Even with pitching and chipping, remember that the distance between you and the flag or back of the green may be greatly distorted. As you play into the green, that twenty yards or so of putting green in front of the flag may visually be squashed down to such an extent that it appears to be only a matter of a few feet. This is why the majority of people continually leave the ball short in pitching and chipping. If you are pitching a ball with the flag right back on the green, the distance behind the flag tends to be foreshortened so much that the flag may look very much closer to the back of the green than it really is. This may intimidate you into playing a cautious shot, several feet short. If you view the

The aspiring tournament player will find it helpful to plot his distances and positioning from the flag for shots to the green. If clubbing is accurate and the shots well hit the pattern of shots will be centred around the flag. For the majority of golfers the positioning would be severely skewed well short of the flag, both with the long game and short game

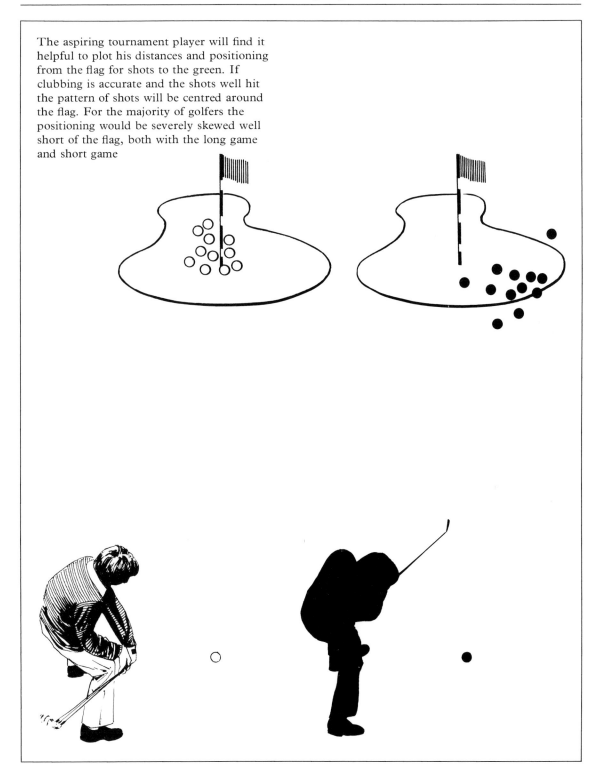

Most golfers are apparently terrified of going past the flag and over the green – terrified as though they were hitting off the edge of the world or landing amongst man-eating tigers. In reality there is probably nothing to be afraid of except fear of the unknown

shot from the side, you will get a far truer picture of the distance you really have to cover. Never be afraid of distance beyond the flag and always try to fight any fear of what may be just beyond the hole until you really do know what is there.

So remember in judging distance the following keys. First, always try to make every shot pass the flag in average conditions. Second, remember that ten yards short equals ten yards to the side and that ten yards short is one club wrong. Third, never ever make a club selection until you are actually at the ball; never before you reach it. Finally, remember that distance on a green appears greatly foreshortened so that the area just in front of the flag and the area beyond the flag are likely to be visually compressed. Good distance in hitting into the green is just as important as good direction. It just isn't so noticeable.

8 The Finesse Game

All the faculties of the golfing mind are brought into play in the finesse game. Many golfers work relatively hard at their golf on the driving range and to a certain extent master the long game. However, although the short game should be very much easier than the long game – requiring relatively little physical ability – this is part of the game that most players ignore and in fact where most fail.

The finesse game comprises not only pitching, chipping and putting but also bunker shots and the general recovery and extra little shots which make up the repertoire of the good player. As in the long game, the physical problems are relatively few and minor, and the difficulties most players encounter are purely problems of the mind. It is once again worth reciting the general principle that the object of each and every shot is to play the ball from A to B. The object with all the short shots is to put the ball down the hole or at least as close as possible to the hole. The central key is therefore ball control; what happens in the swing is purely and simply aimed at making the clubhead execute the path that is most likely to send the ball in the desired direction and the required distance.

Chipping

The most straightforward of the little shots round the green is the simple run-up shot from the edge of the green – the chip. The basic principle of this shot is that the ball is lofted a little way through the air, just to negotiate any fluffy grass round the green, and is then allowed to run right up to the hole. The ideal approach to playing these shots is to think of them as being very much like a putt but with a lofted club. Ideally the shots should be played with a 6 or 7 iron. The reason for adopting one or other of these clubs is that the length of the swing is very similar to that with a putter and therefore easy for most players to judge, while any error in striking the ball is unlikely to be very significant. Players who try to play these shots with a wedge will always find that the swing has to be longer than necessary and that any error in the strike produces either a poorly fluffed shot or one that runs much too far.

The object of the swing is to produce a shallow, saucer-shaped arc to the clubhead path, simply brushing the little piece of grass on which the ball sits, getting the clubhead to the very bottom of the ball, sending it lofting through the air and running on to the target. There should be no question of picking the club up and chopping down into the ball. The action is very much a stroke, not a stab. To produce the desired clubhead path, the club should be held a few inches down the grip, depending slightly on the player's height, the ball fairly well back in the feet and the hands slightly ahead of the clubhead in order to ensure that the contact is clean. The loft of the club is in this way reduced from its usual angle, the 7 iron perhaps sitting like a 6 iron and the 6 like a 5. This encourages the ball to travel forwards and produces a consistent roll as it lands. As we shall see in all the finesse shots, weight is concentrated on the left foot, and in this case, as in most of the others, the feet can be turned round slightly towards the target – which encourages the player to be very much target-oriented. Really this is just like throwing a ball. In throwing the ball towards the target you would naturally adopt this sort of position with the feet slightly turned towards the target.

For the player of a relatively high handicap it is important to ensure with this shot that the hands stay leading the clubhead as the ball is struck, without any tendency for the left arm and left wrist to stop moving and to fold up through impact. The longer-handicap player therefore needs to adopt what feels to be a relatively rigid position, with the left arm stiff and very much in control. This standard of player needs to work hard at keeping the left arm moving through impact, enabling the wrist to stay firm and in control. The feeling should be one of moving the clubhead through a low, shallow, symmetrical arc, simply nipping the little piece of grass on which the ball sits so that the clubhead strikes the ball fully and lofts it

neatly into the air. As the player improves, and there is less likelihood of the left arm stopping and the left wrist crumpling through impact, the arms can be relaxed very slightly. In this swing the arms should still move very much as a unit, without any independent breaking of the wrists and without allowing the clubhead to pass the hands through impact.

The top-class golfer usually plays the chip shot in an entirely different way, with the arms and wrists relaxed, the swing being made by a tiny hand and wrist movement which produces maximum feel and every likelihood of holing quite a fair proportion of chip shots.

Controlling distance with these shots can be a problem. Obviously the intention is to get the ball as close as possible so not only direction but distance is important. One crucial point is the positioning of the ball on the clubhead. As we saw in Chapter 4, whenever you look down at the ball and clubhead the ball will almost always

Below: Jill Thornhill showing the essentials in chipping; that is to keep firmness in the left wrist, with weight favouring the left foot. Backswing and throughswing are of virtually identical length

Facing page: The top-class golfer will usually chip predominantly with the hands and wrists for added feel, nipping the ball neatly from the top of the ground – *not* hitting down into it – and playing the ball nearer the toe of the club than in the long game for additional sensitivity. Taking the flag out for chips tends to focus the mind, make the mental approach more positive and encourage an increasing number of chip-ins

appear to be closer to the toe of the club than it really is. This distortion arises because the eyes are not directly over the ball. In chipping, in particular, it is essential to get the ball in the right place. In the long shots you want to strike the ball from the middle of the club in order to obtain maximum power. In chipping you want to obtain maximum finesse and control, so the ball should be played nearer the toe of the club than in the long shots. By moving the ball on to the toe in this way you will usually find that there is a dramatically different feeling as the ball comes off the clubhead. It is well worth experimenting with. Any player who plays the ball too near the centre or heel of the club will usually find that the ball springs off in an uncontrollable manner and it is very difficult to play short enough shots.

In order to control the distance of the shots the length of the swing must in turn be varied. For most players it is not difficult to produce a relatively long chip, but what is difficult is the very short one. Most players feel insecure when having to play a very small shot and find it hard to swing the club through a short enough distance. The practice technique for chipping should therefore be to try chipping the ball just a matter of a few yards, perhaps five or six yards, so that the player learns to play the stroke and to have confidence in getting the ball airborne even though the clubhead is swung through only a very short distance. Try to be fully aware of the distance you are swinging the clubhead, keeping it within your peripheral vision on backswing and throughswing. The general tendency is to swing the club too far in the backswing, decelerating into impact, instead of keeping the two halves symmetrical.

Some players like to judge distance by gauging where the ball should land and judging the way it rolls the rest of the distance. Other

Left: In playing a short pitch always choose a positive target to land on, look back at the ball, but retain a positive image of your landing spot. Never allow thoughts to become negative – of dribbling the ball in the bunker or thinning it across the green – or this becomes the instruction you will follow

players prefer to think of the overall distance, simply judging the overall loft and run of the ball without any idea of where the ball has to touch down first. In many ways it is therefore helpful to use the same club for all chip shots. The only time to change clubs is where the ratio of desired carry to run is quite wrong for a 7 iron; using a more lofted club will produce a little more carry yet less run. Using predominantly the same club encourages perfect control with the ball. The clubhead, after all, has to become as sensitive as your fingertips; if you were to roll the ball you would have a very good idea of the ball coming off the tips of your fingers, which would be quite sensitive. You need to develop the same sensitivity with your chipping club.

The chip

1.   **Concentrate on producing a shallow, saucer-shaped arc with the clubhead, and the movements of body and legs should fall into place.**

2.   **Work at creating sensitivity in the fingertips and club by playing the ball towards the toe of the club.**

3.   **Bear in mind that the problem for most people is in producing a short enough swing for the tiny shots – backswing and throughswing of equal lengths.**

4.   **Be as positive with chipping as you are in putting, taking the flag out for shortish chips, and you will soon find yourself holing a few.**

Short pitching

As you move further away from the green, you gradually need a shot which has to carry over more fluffy grass or trouble and roll a comparatively short distance. At some stage, therefore, it is necessary to change from a chip shot to a short pitch. What is important is that you don't get caught between the two, playing a shot which is neither one thing nor the other. For playing the short pitch my choice of clubs would usually be the sand iron. After all, if you want to loft the ball through the air you might as well use the most lofted club you have. *Using the sand iron in preference to the pitching wedge also enables you to pitch the ball further over the trouble area, the ball pulling up more quickly.* Many players try to play pitch shots with a 9 iron or pitching wedge; this entails landing the ball very close to the edge of the bunker and gives insufficient space for the ball to stop. One of the most crucial little shots in the game is the short up-and-over pitch which is made from just behind a small bunker or bank, perhaps ten or twenty yards. This should be played in an entirely different manner from the longer pitch and, although both types of shot are generally referred to as pitching, there are two distinct techniques for the little shot and for the longer one.

In playing the short pitch with the sand iron, try to determine whether or not the whole of the ball is sitting above the ground. However bare the lie, if the whole ball sits above the ground, the shot can be played in a very simple manner without using any hand and wrist action but

---

The short, up-and-over pitch is best played with a sand iron. Providing the whole ball sits above the ground – however tight the lie – the shot is executed by keeping the arms and club moving as a unit, back and forwards in a simple pendulum arc, *not* stiffly from the shoulders, but using the legs and body to produce the movement and keeping the wrists stiff and lifeless. Move the legs to make the arms move

instead relying on a sort of pendulum style whereby the whole object is to brush the ground on which the ball sits, the loft of the club simply popping the ball up into the air. If any of the ball is below the level of the ground, then it is necessary to use a more difficult, wristy shot which requires considerably greater control and is certainly far more difficult to play under pressure.

In order to play the simple up-and-over shot, the sand iron should be set squarely to the target, the shaft of the club coming directly up towards the player and the hands placed several inches down the grip of the club, arms hanging straight. As in the chip shot, the feet are turned slightly towards the target and the player is thus enabled to concentrate and focus on the target. The shot is executed by keeping the arms and club very much as a unit and by moving the club back and forwards in a simple pendulum arc, using the legs and body to produce the movement and keeping the wrists still and lifeless. The end of the shaft of the club should start very close in to the body and if the shot is executed correctly stays close in to the body throughout. *The feeling of the swing should be one of moving the legs in order to make the arms move.*

In other words, there is a feeling of pivoting the legs on the backswing and then driving the legs through to the target in the throughswing which leads to the movement of the club. It is not a question of playing a stiff shot from the shoulders.

As the club swings back, the face of the club remains in a relatively shut position – i.e. the face of the club is pointing down at the ground – and as the legs drive through in the throughswing the face of the club points upwards beyond impact, that is, in an open position. The object of the swing is to make the club brush the little piece of ground on which the ball sits, and the loft of the club will float it quite high and softly into the air. There is no need to have any feeling of cutting the ball up or lifting it in any way.

In order to play these shots, you should first choose the spot on which you want the ball to land. Do bear in mind at this point that distance tends to be foreshortened and a spot which to you looks to be the correct landing spot may when seen from the side be quite obviously too short. If time permits, look at the shot from the side to assess the correct landing spot. Then have two or three practice swings to enable you to feel the correct depth of the swing. It is

important at this point to have the feeling of making the clubhead brush the ground to enable it to get to the very bottom of the ball as the swing takes place. When you set up to the ball it is important to have in your mind a very clear mental picture of the spot on which you want the ball to land. What too easily happens is that the player is unable to obtain such a mental picture and is therefore forced into looking up too quickly in order to try to see the landing spot as the ball is struck. Ensure that you produce a vivid picture of where you want the ball to land, look down at the ball and then concentrate on brushing the little spot on which the ball sits. Try in all these short shots to stay looking down as long as you can and certainly until the ball has landed; don't look up in the vain hope of trying to see ball and target at the same time.

What so easily tends to happen in these little shots is that players become negative over their approach to them. Many a golfer faced with a little shot over a bunker, certainly if under any pressure, will often allow negative thoughts to run through his mind, thinking not so much of where he wants the ball to land as what he hopes he doesn't do with the shot. It is all too easy to have a picture of the ball dribbling along the ground into the bunker in front of you. If you do this, bear in mind as we have seen earlier that this becomes your set of instructions to the brain and the brain will tune into a programme for dribbling the ball in front of you. So think positively, conjure up a positive picture of where you want the ball to land and concentrate on producing the right depth of contact in the shot. Block out any irrational fear of what is beyond the flag and be bold.

Obviously this kind of shot is much easier the lusher the grass on which the ball sits. However, even from a bare lie, the shot can be executed in

Neil Coles playing a long pitch, weight favouring the left foot throughout, the wrists cocking very early in the backswing, but then punching down and through into a short, punchy finish. The ball is attacked from the inside, *not* with an outside-in, cutting action. (Notice his very individual style of addressing the ball in the neck of the club)

exactly the same way. It is simply a question of judging it more accurately, ensuring that the clubhead brushes the ground and that the depth of the swing is judged within an eighth of an inch or so.

Having learnt to play these short shots, learn to choose between them and to use them correctly. The first choice for most people should usually be to putt the ball if possible, looking to the chip as the second choice and pitching the ball only if absolutely necessary. Bear in mind that the simplest way of playing up a bank is to putt or run the ball, and always look to these as the safer alternatives.

Long pitching

The method for short pitching described above is applicable only for shots of perhaps ten to twenty-five or thirty yards. Beyond this distance it is necessary to produce a shot where there is some wrist action in the backswing in order to create sufficient power to send the ball on target. Many golfers, however, try to adopt the long-pitching method for short shots, setting up too much power in the backswing and then having to curb this power in an unsatisfactory manner in the throughswing. *The long-pitching technique should be adopted for the short shots only where the ball is sitting in a bad lie, slightly below the level of the ground, and where it is necessary to squeeze the ball out and to use the hands in order to create height.*

In setting up to play the long pitch, the ball should be played back in the feet, slightly behind the centre of the stance, so that the hands are ahead of the clubhead and the effective loft of the clubhead is reduced slightly. The shot can be played with sand iron, pitching

wedge or 9 iron. Each is played in exactly the same way and indeed the shot can then be developed to produce a punch shot with the longer irons. The feet are once again turned towards the target, but the shoulders are kept in a square position. Weight is again concentrated on the left side in order to produce a downward contact, striking the ball and then the turf beyond it. The grip is the conventional golf grip, gripping two or three inches down the club, depending on the height of the player.

This is one of the more unusual shots in golf, in that backswing and throughswing are *not* mirror images of each other as they are in almost all other shots. In the backswing the wrists should be cocked quite naturally and very early, but at the same time ensuring that the clubhead is swung back on the inside of the ball–target line. There should be no question of lifting the club steeply in an outside–in direction. The clubhead must still be swung back on the inside and the ball must be attacked from the inside, not, as many amateurs imagine, with a cutting, out-to-in attack. The hands are used quite early and freely in the takeaway, but it is essential for weight then to be transferred well on to the left side and the arms and wrists to stay firm through impact, so that at the end of the swing the club is pointing out towards the target, with the back of the left wrist and the left arm firm to produce a punching attack. What too easily happens is that by using the wrists in the backswing the player is then encouraged to allow the wrists to fold up in the throughswing. Good pitching is not simply a question of producing a slow, loose version of the full swing. It is a definite technique all of its own, requiring the hands and wrists to be used freely in the backswing but then to stay firm and in control in the throughswing. Once again it is important to produce a clear mental picture of where the ball is to land, keeping this picture firmly in the mind through impact rather than looking up in an effort to see the target at the same time as the ball is struck.

Good judgement of distance in pitching is largely a question of practice. As we saw in the previous chapter, one of the downfalls of many players is that they allow the thought process to change from a reflex type of thinking to a slow-speed type of thinking under competitive conditions. In pitching, in particular, it is essential to determine exactly how you are going to judge distance. Are you going to analyse it very carefully or are you going to rely on high-speed, reflex thought? Whatever you do in practice you must also do in play. Frequently, again, players will pitch at one speed in practice or in relatively light-hearted play but will then become slower and more analytical as soon as they move into a competitive environment. As a rule the experienced player will be at his best with pitching if he relies on one or, at the most, two glances at the target and executes the shot spontaneously with no forced judgement of distance. *Make absolutely certain with pitching that your approach to this shot remains the same, either always taking plenty of time during practice or forcing yourself to be relatively spontaneous in a championship.* Bear in mind that distance on the

Lee Trevino, one of the great exponents of the punch shot. The wrists having worked early and freely in the backswing punch through into a short, firm finish, driving the ball out firmly on-target

green and particularly round the hole tends to be foreshortened quite considerably, and work at a bold approach which aims at making each shot pass the flag.

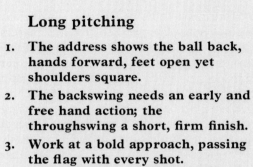

Long pitching

1. **The address shows the ball back, hands forward, feet open yet shoulders square.**
2. **The backswing needs an early and free hand action; the throughswing a short, firm finish.**
3. **Work at a bold approach, passing the flag with every shot.**
4. **Only adopt this method for a short pitch when a really bad lie necessitates.**

The punch shot

One of the most useful tactics in windy conditions is to play a firm punch shot with an iron that travels relatively low but with standard distance. The shot, which can be played with anything from a 3 iron upwards, is approached in very much the same way as a long pitch; the ball is positioned back in the feet, the backswing is made with an early and free hand action, but the followthrough is short and controlled. In playing this shot you should work at controlling the clubface through impact in order to have the feeling of punching the ball on target. Many players find that they are inconsistent with direction in these shots, either in playing the ball back in the stance and thus allowing it to be pushed out to the right, or in stopping the swing with a short, punchy followthrough so that the hands turn excessively through impact and the clubface closes. Most players need to feel that

they are stopping the shot with a very firm left arm through impact so that the clubface is held square as the ball is struck. When played well, distance equates surprisingly closely to a full shot with the same club.

Bunker shots

Almost all professional golfers will tell you that bunker shots from relatively good lies, at least, are easier than conventional pitch shots. The club golfer, by contrast, tends to be frightened by bunker shots. The more intimidating he finds them, the more likely he is to be drawn towards the bunker!

The first point about good bunker play is that it is essential to have the right type of club. A good sand wedge should have the leading edge slightly ahead of the hosel of the club, a well-rounded leading edge which enables you to open the clubface where necessary, and with the lie of the club slightly flatter than the pitching wedge, ensuring that the club sits flat to the sand as it moves through impact. The first shot to consider is the simple splash shot, which should be played when the ball is in a fairly good lie in the bunker, for a shot of anything from five to thirty yards. The principle of this shot is that the clubhead is swung back and through, splashing out a handful of sand around the ball so that the ball pops out with it. The ball itself is *not* struck by the clubhead. The whole attention has to be focused on the sand. In order to achieve this, the clubhead should be set as close to the sand as possible, approximately an inch and a half behind the ball, with the eyes focused on a spot an inch or so behind the ball, the stance slightly open and the weight if anything concentrated on the left foot. The whole swing is like a fairly full, slow swing with any of the iron clubs, concentrating on picking the club up fairly steeply both in the backswing and again in the throughswing to produce a U-shaped arc. Usually, the slower the swing, the better are the results. The eyes should be focused firmly on the spot in the sand behind the ball and the feeling has to be one of splashing the sand out. Many golfers realize that the clubhead has to enter the sand just behind the ball but forget that it also has to be swung on out and up the other side. Concentrate in the bunker shots on the swing through the ball and simply have the

Greg Norman demonstrates the basic splash shot, stance open, weight favouring the left foot, eyes and club set an inch or two behind the ball, with the wrists breaking freely in the backswing and splashing right through the sand to a really full, relaxed followthrough

feeling of splashing the sand forward and out. Don't simply bury the clubhead in the sand.

In order to play the shot accurately the clubface should also be slightly opened – in other words, it should face out to the right with increased loft. This opening of the clubface must take place before the club is gripped. Since golf grips are usually designed to be not perfectly round but slightly egg-shaped, the grip may feel slightly awkward once the clubface is opened and the club takes up a different position in the palm of the hand. Ensure too that the ball remains central or towards the toe of the club as the face is opened. Frequently a bunker shot assumed to be a top is an undetected socket caused by careless opening of the clubface and mispositioning of the ball. In opening the clubface in this way, it is almost certain that the ball will always pop out slightly to the right of your target. For this reason the stance should be aimed round to the left and you may need to feel that the whole swing has to go slightly left of target in order to produce the correct direction for the shot. Many people describe this as an 'out-to-in swing'. This tends to be a confusing phrase in that it often leads people to believe that the swing has to be out-to-in in relation to

the line of the body. This is not necessary and is only likely to lead to catching the shot off the socket. All that has to be done is to aim the swing slightly left of target in order to allow for the fact that the clubface is set to the right. With experience you will gradually find how much you need to offset one against the other. The swing is a full, very slow swing. Concentrate on looking at the spot in the sand behind the ball and simply think of splashing out the handful of sand, with emphasis on the forward-and-through movement.

To control distance in the bunker there are several approaches you can take. The first is to vary the amount of sand you splash out, looking closer towards the ball for the longer shot and therefore hoping to take less sand, and looking further behind the ball for the shorter shot and therefore hoping to take more sand. An alternative approach is to vary the angle of the clubface, opening it more for a short shot and less for a longer shot. Alternatively you can simply adapt the length and speed of the swing in order to produce finesse and to judge distance accordingly. What is important is to decide at which point you should actually try to control distance. The majority of club golfers

are relatively unsophisticated in the distance they produce with bunker shots. It is far better in many instances to be satisfied with a repetitive ten-yard shot that serves the purpose for most shots round the green than to try to vary distance before you are really capable of so doing. For the player who is capable of varying distance, probably the easiest way of producing a slightly shorter shot is to try to take slightly more sand, and the easiest way of producing a longer shot is to play a conventional splash shot but with a squarer clubface. Most professional golfers will try to play a particularly short bunker shot by cutting down the swing and playing a very soft, delicate shot. This is difficult for all but the really top-class player, and many golfers come unstuck when trying to be too delicate with a tiny bunker shot.

Bunker shots

1. **The most difficult mental problem in bunker shots is one of focusing on the sand behind the ball and *not* looking at the ball.**
2. **Work at a full, *ridiculously slow* swing, remembering that the slower the swing the easier the clubhead will penetrate the sand.**
3. **Open the clubface before gripping the club and simply aim left to allow for this.**

Another shot which tends to cause difficulty is the one where the ball is completely buried. This really should give no particular concern: the shot is fairly easy to execute; it merely requires a good nerve and plenty of brute force. When the ball is attacked it should be a little further back in the stance than usual, the hands should be slightly ahead of the ball and you should have the feeling of lifting the club in the backswing and then chopping down through the sand and ball in the throughswing. The eyes should be focused perhaps half an inch behind the ball.

The fairway bunker shot similarly should cause relatively few problems. The main point is not to be too ambitious over your choice of clubs. Do be absolutely certain that the clubhead has sufficient loft to get the ball over any bank in front of you. Even many professionals have come unstuck at an unfortunate moment in a tournament by being too ambitious in their choice of clubbing. In order to play the long bunker shot you have to look at the lie of the ball. If any of the ball is below the level of the sand, the shot should be approached in very

---

In playing a bunker shot the clubface is opened to add loft and backswing. To offset this the stance and swing are aimed left of target and the ball pops out on-target. The swing does not need to be out-to-in in relation to the line of the body. Just aim a little left to offset the open clubface

much the same way as the short- or medium-iron shot would be tackled, having the hands slightly ahead of the ball and hitting fractionally down on the ball, taking the ball and then the sand beyond it. If, on the other hand, the whole of the ball is sitting above the sand the shot should be tackled differently. This time it is important that the eyes should be focused on the back or even slightly towards the top of the ball, concentrating on picking it cleanly off the top of the sand and not taking any sand at all.

In the downhill bunker shot it is essential to set the weight as much as possible on the left foot and to keep the right shoulder high, the line of the shoulders following the slope of the ground. The backswing can then be very steep, the downswing going down the slope beyond the ball

The downhill bunker shot

Perhaps the most difficult of all bunker shots is the one where the ball just dribbles into the back of the bunker and is left on a downhill slope. As in all downhill shots there are two main problems. First the effective loft of the club is reduced and it is therefore difficult to get much height. Second, it is all too easy to catch the ground behind the ball and not to have a clean contact. In order to overcome the second of these problems, it is essential to play the ball very much towards the right foot, *setting the weight as much as possible on the left foot so that the line of the shoulders follows the slope of the ground*. This address position may feel very awkward and slightly off balance, but it does enable the club to be swung up and down the slope without scuffing the sand behind the ball. The clubface should be set very slightly open; and the player must ensure that the ball is on the middle or toe of the club and not too near the socket, and must concentrate on swinging the club up in the backswing and then following through down and beyond the ball in the throughswing. The eyes should once again be focused approximately an inch behind the ball and should be kept firmly focused there through impact. What one has to bear in mind is that the effective loft of the club is reduced quite dramatically and as a result the ball will travel with very little height. Do not be too ambitious in aiming to get the ball over the highest part of the bank. Be prepared for it to go off fairly low and also for it to run several yards as it lands on the green. A difficult shot to play, but, providing the set-up is correct and the line of the shoulders follows the slope, it is at least far more possible than most players imagine.

The psychology of putting

In many ways putting is a game all of its own. There are some golfers who are well below average so far as their long game and pitching are concerned and yet putt to exceptionally high standards. Other golfers have a long game of top-class level and yet fail miserably as soon as they get on to the greens.

Ability at putting is almost certainly linked with having a good eye for the ball and being able to 'see' the line to the hole. As a rule, the top-class player who is not a good putter usually suffers from inherent lack of ability to see his way to the target clearly. For exactly the opposite reasons some players can putt exceptionally well, while failing to conform to all general theories of this aspect of the game.

Style at putting is relatively unimportant. The usually accepted rules of technique are frequently broken by some of the world's top putters. However, the basic principles agreed upon by most professionals are that the eyes should be directly over the ball or, if anything, slightly inside the ball–target line, while the hands should be very slightly ahead of the ball. The putter should move low to the ground on both backswing and throughswing. Some professionals suggest that the putter should move perfectly straight back and through with a short putt, while others maintain that the putter must always be brought back slightly on the inside of the ball–target line. Grips too can vary considerably, while the individual styles in stance and ball position show that there are really no strict rules to which the player should adhere. The main point about putting is almost certainly developing a good eye for reading the

greens, having the basic ability to see the line to the hole and aim perfectly along it, while also developing a repetitive stroke and a reliable contact.

The difference one sees in putting styles provides an important lesson. The crux of good putting is largely to disentangle oneself from theory and too many thoughts of the body, and instead concentrate wholeheartedly on getting the ball into the hole. If one can focus on this, and this alone, it goes a long way towards guiding the body and clubhead to produce the right movements.

The mental approach to putting is as important – if not more important – than the mental approach to all other aspects of the game. It looks as though it should be so simple and yet of course it isn't. It seems ludicrous that the professional golfer can drive a ball 250 yards or so within a few feet of where he wants it and yet can fail to put the ball in the hole from a mere four or five feet. It is so easy to lose one's nerve, become negative, obsessive about style and the putting stroke, and so on. Positive thinking is essential. The player must visualize the ball

Gary Player with his distinctive style of putting showing the reverse overlap grip, perhaps the most common putting grip

diving into the hole before each putt, resisting any tendency for his mind to become sidetracked into thoughts of the ball missing. A split second of doubt, with an image of the ball veering away to right or left, is disastrous, usually giving the brain a wrong instruction and producing an inadequate putt.

Mental rehearsal of the putting stroke can certainly bear fruit. The player who is not a particularly good short putter is well advised regularly to spend a few minutes each day thinking of the putting stroke and imagining the ball rolling towards the hole. This helps not only to groove the feeling of the putting stroke but also to boost confidence. In many ways such mental practice can do almost as much good as physical practice. Every time the brain visualizes the correct movements this strengthens the muscle-memory programme and improves the likelihood of success. The key, however, is largely one of concentrating on the ball and the hole and working hard at making the ball do exactly what you want it to.

In putting, as in the long game, good judgement of distance is crucial, especially with putts from the edge of the green. The same principles again apply. The ground nearest to the hole tends to be foreshortened and this part of the distance is often very difficult to assess. No doubt you will frequently have hit a long putt from the edge of the green and thought the ball had rolled up within a foot or eighteen inches of the hole, only to find as you walked up closer to it that the ball was considerably further away than you first thought. That six-foot area – three feet short and three feet past the flag – tends to be extremely difficult to 'see' accurately. For this reason it may well help to walk the length of the putt and perhaps look at it from the side in order to gain a better overall impression of the distance. This sideways look at the putt can also help to provide a true picture of the uphill and downhill slope between ball and hole.

In judging distance with long putts, it is a good routine to have two or three practice swings, not so much to practise the stroke itself as to assess the distance of the shot. You may find it useful to look at the hole while you have these two or three practice swings, gauging the length of the backswing, visualizing the strike with the ball and then imagining the ball running to the hole. A couple of practice strokes followed by a practice swing of the same length with the eyes focused on the ground may well help your overall judgement of distance and

David Graham with a very orthodox putting style, putter travelling low both back and through

your feel for the way in which the ball is likely to roll. You may also find that as a practice technique it helps to roll a ball the length of the green with your hand to try to feel the relationship between releasing the ball with your fingertips and striking the ball with a putter head. In order to judge distance really well, the sensitivity in your fingers has to be translated to the end of the putter, giving you perfect feel of the ball leaving the clubhead.

Players who are poor long putters often fail to make a consistent contact with the ball. In chipping, it is essential to get to the very bottom of the ball and the clubhead will usually just nip the little piece of grass on which the ball sits. In putting, the action is somewhat different, for the clubhead should come as close as possible to the bottom of the ball without actually scuffing the ground. Unfortunately it is all too easy to strike the ball with the putter head a considerable distance from the ground and consequently from the bottom of the ball. If this happens, the contact is likely to vary from putt to putt and the distance too will be erratic. With the player who is a good chipper and a bad putter, the root of the trouble is often this type of problem concerning depth of contact.

Being a good putter is largely a question of having a few key concepts on which to rely. Some players like to think of their long putts as though they were trying to get the ball into a circle perhaps two feet in radius around the hole. The player then ignores the hole itself, so that the ball can be left reliably dead for the next stroke. Some players do this by thinking of a white circle on the ground; others like to imagine a huge bucket into which the ball has to drop, and other players no doubt have their own visual images to give them a suitable target. In allowing for a borrow to one side or the other, some players think of the whole curve of the putt and aim to start the ball off on this curve and to visualize it bending away to the hole. Others prefer to choose a definite spot to the

Hubert Green shows his own very personal style of putting, hands forward, crouching over the ball

side of the hole and to visualize banging the ball straight at that. Another excellent concept is to imagine you have a tee peg as your target a few inches to the appropriate side of the hole, practising on the putting green to a tee peg, rather than a hole, to reinforce this idea. A useful concept with short putts is to visualize a tee peg stuck in the ground just at the back of the hole and to putt the ball firmly at this to ensure that there is no risk of leaving it short.

Developing a good putting stroke is important. Many top-class players practise their short-putting stroke by swinging the putter backwards and forwards along another club shaft or in between two club shafts in order to ensure that the putter really is kept travelling in a straight line. A similarly worthwhile exercise for developing a good stroke is to practise striking the ball with the name on the ball uppermost and pointing directly at the hole. A good stroke will show the name rolling over and over in a straight line, not wobbling to left or right. Developing a good putting stroke in this way must take place on the practice green. Once one gets out on to the golf course the same principles as in the long game apply. Technique must be largely forgotten; you must trust that it stays with you, but give yourself time to think of the shots in hand and to concentrate on making the ball do what you want it to.

What is important when you get out on to the golf course is to have a putting technique that stands up to pressure. It is essential for the tournament player to adopt a very definite method for putting which does not alter under pressure. We saw in the last chapter just how easy it is for the thought processes to change in different golfing situations. Just the same can happen with putting. The stroke on the practice green is likely to be simple and repetitive. With a little bit of pressure the hands start fidgeting, the odd, unnecessary practice swing is added, one looks up at the hole a couple more times than usual, and the pattern breaks down. Develop not only a style of putting but a routine of putting and stick to it through thick and thin for the whole round of golf. Set your hands on the club and don't fidget. Have one practice swing or two practice swings or whatever, and be repetitive and consistent. Address the ball and look up once or even twice or three times. It doesn't matter how many, but do the same each time. Don't fall into the trap of trying that little bit harder and having an extra look. It serves only to confuse and to reduce spontaneity and confidence. Think positively and putt with an unerring self-belief.

Understanding slopes

Players frequently have difficulty playing shots from sloping lies. Very often this is a question not of poor technique but rather of conceptual problems. Once understood, sloping lies should cause relatively little extra difficulty.

In the shot where the ball is above your feet, the ball will also be further away from you and the swing necessarily goes round on a more horizontal plane. This should happen quite automatically without any particular attention from you. The swing becomes more like a baseball swing, catching the ball from somewhere about knee level. You may like to hold the club slightly further down from the end of the grip but this is not essential. The swing travels round further in both the backswing and the throughswing and if struck correctly the ball will nearly always bend away to the left in flight. What you should also remember – and this is where most club golfers come unstuck – is that the ball not only curves to the left in mid-air but is also likely to land on ground that is sloping away to the left. On landing, the ball will very often kick well away to the left, and most club golfers fail to allow enough to the right in their aiming. The execution of the shot should be relatively simple – certainly for anyone who is prone to slicing. The shot is more likely to be a problem for the professional golfer who if anything has a tendency to draw the ball.

When the player is standing above the ball exactly the opposite problem is encountered: the ball comes closer to the feet and the body is necessarily bent over more. This produces a much higher, steeper plane of swing and the real problem for the club golfer is usually one of staying down through impact. Most club golf-

ers and, indeed, many top-class players have a tendency to look away from the ball fractionally early, and this is most likely to occur in the kind of shot where the ball is well below the feet. The main point is usually to concentrate on staying down well. The second point is that, with the ball very close into the feet like this, there is often a tendency to fall forward, losing balance through impact. Consequently the bottom of the swing is very often brought down a couple of inches too far away from the feet and there is a definite tendency for many club golfers to catch the ball from the neck of the club. It is not a question of standing further from the ball at address but rather one of being absolutely certain of maintaining balance through impact. Those are the difficult points of technique – staying down and maintaining balance. As far as the shot itself is concerned, there is a tendency for the ball to fade away to the right, and, since the ball will often be landing on ground that slopes in the same direction, it will kick further away when it lands. In this case it is essential to aim well away to the left of the target, again bearing in mind that most club golfers fail to allow sufficient width in their aiming. Always tend to over-compensate when standing above the ball. Try to analyse your own shots and you will almost certainly see a pattern of failing to keep far enough to the left. Again choose a definite target and don't be halfhearted about the shot.

The concept to remember in these two shots is that the ball curves in the air the same way as it would run on the ground. When the player stands below the ball, for a right-handed player the ball will be rolling away to the left; it will therefore curve away to the left in the air. Conversely, when the player stands above the ball, it will roll away to the right; it therefore curves away to the right in mid-air.

Playing a ball from an uphill lie is often the easiest shot for the club golfer. Particularly with

---

In standing below the ball the swing naturally becomes flatter, the ball tending to hook away to the left. Bear in mind that it will quite probably be landing on ground sloping the same way, so allow for the ball to kick left too

the longer club, the slight elevation on the ground tends to increase the effective loft of the club and will help get the ball airborne. For this reason the long irons and fairway woods are often easier to use from a slightly uphill slope than they are from a flat lie. This is true of a very slight incline. Once the slope becomes at all steep, however, there is a problem of using the feet correctly and of maintaining balance. From a steep uphill slope it is often very difficult to get the weight transferred properly on to the left foot in the throughswing, and there is an awkward tendency to hang back on the right foot. For the long shot from a fairly steep slope the rule is probably to allow yourself to stand out at right angles from the ground so that the line of the shoulders follows the slope of the ground. In this way one need not attempt to get on to the left foot through impact. This necessitates, however, a compensation in the flight of the ball, which will almost always tend to go off extremely high and bend away to the left. The player should therefore allow for this by taking plenty of club and, if anything, aiming to the right of the green. Where the slope of the ground is not so severe or when a medium or shorter iron is used, the best approach is to keep the weight centred rather on the left foot, i.e. leaning into the slope; concentrating on staying on the left foot through impact and punching the club into the slope. This will make the flight of the ball not very different from a normal shot and, if there is any tendency to sway to the left at impact, may even produce a shot which pushes away slightly to the right of target.

Playing a shot downhill is again one of the more difficult shots for the club golfer. In any shot from a downhill slope there are two problems. The first is to make sure that the ball is struck cleanly without catching the ground behind it. The second is that the effective loft of the club is reduced according to the steepness of the slope.

In standing above the ball, it will naturally be brought closer to the feet, producing a more upright swing than normal. It is essential to maintain balance through impact, the ball slicing away to the right quite sharply

In order to produce a good, clean contact from a downhill lie it is essential to understand the principles involved. *The crucial point is to adopt a stance in which the body is positioned out at right angles from the slope so that the shoulders follow the line of the slope, with the right shoulder carried as high as possible.* This may feel extremely awkward, as the balance on the left foot seems precarious. None the less, from this type of set-up it is comparatively simple to swing the clubhead up and down the line of the slope without digging into the ground behind the ball. In order to give even more chance of a solid contact, the ball should be positioned well back in the stance – in other words towards the right foot. This again gives an added likelihood of striking the ball without catching the ground behind it.

Many players understand the principle of having the ball further back in the feet on a downhill lie but often fail to appreciate the importance of having the shoulders following the slope of the ground. Many comparatively good golfers and even young professionals often fall into the trap of leaving the ball well back and yet lowering the right shoulder into an unsuitable position. *The higher the right shoulder is carried at address, the steeper the backswing and steeper the downswing.* The swing should now follow the slope of the ground for as long as possible, producing a steep, high backswing but, even more important, having the feeling of following down beyond the ball in the throughswing. Ideally the clubhead should continue down the slope beyond the ball for a fraction of a second. It may well be that just after the ball is struck the player loses his balance down the hill. This doesn't matter and is certainly a far better tendency than allowing the weight to fall back on to the right foot and so catching the ground behind the ball.

Once the player has set up into a position from which a clean contact can be produced, it is important to analyse what is likely to happen to the flight of the ball. First of all the effective loft of the club is likely to be reduced considerably, so that a 6 or 7 iron may well fly with a trajectory of a 2 or 3 iron. This means that the long irons and the fairway woods may be virtually impossible to use from a downhill slope. Judging distance can be a difficulty because although a 6 iron may fly with a 3 iron's trajectory, it is unlikely to carry as far as a 3 iron, basically because the shaft of the club is shorter and the clubhead speed is consequently not so great. The overall carry on the shot may therefore be about the same as from a flat lie and may even be slightly reduced. What has to be taken into account is the slope of the ground on which the ball is going to land and the probable run of the ball on landing. Another factor that requires compensation in addressing the ball is the direction of the shot. Since the ball is caught further back in the feet, it will usually start a little to the right of target and will then drift even further to the right. In playing any downhill shot it is therefore essential to aim well to the left of the target and allow for this variation in direction.

Sloping lies, once understood, should cause relatively little difficulty. It is largely a question of understanding the principles involved and aiming sufficiently to one side or the other as necessary.

Mastery of the shots of 'the finesse game' is an important part of the player's total golfing education. The shots in themselves are not particularly difficult: the short shots make less physical demands on the player than the long game and the remainder very largely only require understanding to adapt as necessary the standard swing.

9 Playing the Game

Many golfers achieve a relatively high standard of striking the ball but fail to take advantage of this ability in so far as the scoring game is concerned. *The whole essence of golf is an ability to strike the ball from A to B combined with success at achieving as low a score as possible.* A sad lack of awareness of the features and challenge of any particular golf course often inhibits any real progress at the game. Not only does every golf course differ from every other golf course, but no course is ever really identical on two given days: the weather changes; the tee and flag positions are altered; the grass is cut differently. The overall challenge before you in any particular game is an entirely different one.

Playing the course

Some golfers undoubtedly have a far better golfing brain than others do. They can see the problems before them, assess the requirements of any particular hole and any particular shot, and pit their wits against those of the golf-course architect and greenkeeper without a moment's weakness. Others can strike the ball with perfection and still play into the hands of the architect by falling for his tempting bait and failing to notice his subtle snares. Undoubtedly the architects of the world's great golf courses must go into the afterlife knowing they have left a tantalizing challenge, probably never to be truly beaten by generations of would-be opponents. The well-designed golf hole provides a distinct trail of danger zones and safety zones which blend together in such a way that they may require a fairly astute golfing brain to

unravel the architect's web of intrigue. To the connoisseur this is the game at its best. To others the subtleties of his challenge may be totally unappreciated.

The challenges the architect and greenkeeper set up for you take many different forms. They can lure you into trouble, dare you to take stupid risks, frighten you into error or fool you into making the wrong decision.

Let's consider, for example, some classic types of schemes. One of the favourite lures is a position of safety which looks inviting and is straight on line between you and the green. You feel you could hit it so easily. Now that lure may very well be setting you up for the most awkward possible position for the next shot. It may leave you with a long carry, a bunker to negotiate or quite the wrong approach into the green. If you take the bait you get out of position. Or the lure may be beckoning you towards it because it will draw you in much too close to danger. The merest fraction off line and you are away in a ditch or down in a bunker. The greenkeeper may do exactly the same thing. He pops the flag over on one side of the green, ten feet beyond a bunker, and lures you towards the flag so that the slightest imperfection sees you falter.

With experience you must learn not only to spot the likely danger zones but also to understand how the golf-course architect plans to draw you towards them. If there is trouble all down one side of the fairway and not down the other side, how is he trying to drive you towards the trouble? He may be relying on a prevailing wind, or be bending the whole fairway that way so that you bite off a little more than you can chew, or he may frighten you away from the other side of the fairway to lure you away into real snares. The 'frightener' is the sort of hazard that very rarely catches anyone – and wouldn't really be severely destructive if it did – but it is just so cleverly placed and obvious-looking that it sends you away in the opposite direction.

Another of the danger zones is the irresistible dare. The architect's favourite dare is the dogleg where you are either tempted to cut the corner – usually with the result that you leave yourself blocked for the next shot – or where the temptation to try to carry the corner is made virtually irresistible although it is wellnigh impossible to achieve. The eighteenth on the Burma Road at Wentworth is surely one of the most successful. This is a very big two-shot hole, bending to the right quite sharply just past driving length. There isn't a bunker to be seen off the tee. Not only is there a virtually irresistible dare to hug too close to the right to cut off at the most five or ten yards to the green, but there is also some relatively thick, though not usually long, rough down the left. The frightener and the dare work hand in hand to lure many a good player into an impossible blocked position for the second shot, or even to coax him away into the trees.

Another type of dare is the one where a flag is placed just over a bunker, just over a pond or too close to the back of the green for comfort. In doing this the greenkeeper is setting up a particular form of challenge and again literally daring you to get into trouble. He almost certainly knows that one particular dare with the pin position on a certain hole is his most rewarding. In some way it probably tempts and teases you to such an extent that it is virtually impossible to resist the challenge.

> **Learn to spot the lures or dares set up by the architect or greenkeeper and don't be tricked or teased into trouble.**

The illusion is perhaps the most subtle of the danger points. A bunker twenty yards short of the green may look as though it is immediately in front of the green, producing certain dead ground which you fail to take into account. A particularly large bunker or enormous trees may foreshorten the whole distance and trick players into being repeatedly short. Or there may be subtle illusions of slopes, with green and fairway seeming to be so at odds that the player acquires a nervous uncertainty about the terrain. The architect may design his greens to look deceptively short from front to back, again tempting the player to underclub. On a blind hole he may trick you into going in the wrong direction by creating the illusion of trouble down one side and an open invitation down the other. Even when you have experienced the hole on several occasions, the illusion may still take effect.

In order to play good tactical golf it is essential to think out a particular hole and to figure out where the trouble really lies. You need to weigh up the danger zones, understand how the architect proposes to lure you towards them and then try to assess the optimum position, allowing a realistic margin for your own error, but with a definite target in mind for every shot. Not only will this kind of understanding and realization produce a more logical approach to your golf; it will almost certainly enhance your appreciation and enjoyment of the challenge of the course and its design.

Strategic planning

Planning the approach to each hole is a question not only of experience but of realizing the principles involved. Most good golfers are extremely shrewd in their attack on any particular golf hole. In many ways the good golfer gets considerably more enjoyment out of playing on a really good golf course than the club golfer does. Frequently the club golfer fails to realize the exceptional characteristics of a good course, either because the well-placed bunkers fail to impress him or because his mastery of planning the approach to the course is insufficient.

The 18th on the Burma Road at Wentworth presents the player with a typical irresistible dare. The correct line is down the left of the fairway, opening up the second shot from where the good player can just reach the green. The temptation is to hug too close to the trees on the right to cut off distance, resulting in a blocked approach to the green

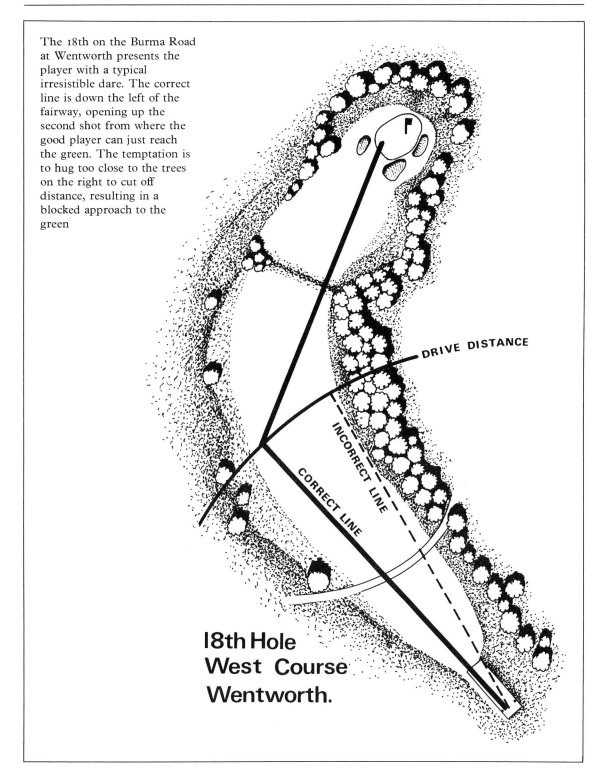

DRIVE DISTANCE

INCORRECT LINE

CORRECT LINE

18th Hole
West Course
Wentworth.

Strategic planning of your attack on every golf hole is essential. Clearly many golf holes, particularly on the average golf course, require relatively little thought. The drive has to be banged down the middle, and the second shot has to be fired into the centre of the green. But on the good championship courses the drive very often has to be angled away from the centre of the fairway if the player is to get into position for the next shot or steer safely away from costly trouble. The drive may not need a full-blooded shot and may well require the player to lay up with a long iron or one of the fairway woods.

One of the main rules for planning your way successfully round the golf course is to be prepared to aim away from the centre of the fairway and also to aim away from the flag if necessary. As you set up on the tee, decide whether there is any particular trouble area on one side of the fairway and also try to assess whether there is any possible driving zone which will open up your shot to the green. If, for example, there is a punishing bunker out on the right-hand side, this may well dictate that you should drive towards the left of the fairway, even with the risk of going into the rough. If you want to drive to the left of the fairway, then you should correctly tee up on the right-hand side of the tee; this encourages you to turn away to the left automatically in the set-up. Conversely, if there is trouble all down the left side of the fairway and you want to aim away to the right, it is generally easier to position yourself on the left-hand side of the tee and thus aim away to the other side. Many club golfers fail to position themselves correctly on the tee and minimize their chances of hitting the correct spot on the fairway. They either rush on to the tee in a thoroughly haphazard way or dive into the footprints and 'teeprints' of the previous player.

> **Be prepared to aim away from the centre of the fairway to keep away from potential trouble. Tee up on the same side as the trouble and you will find it easier to aim away from it.**

The difficult bunker for most club players is one that is positioned to the right of the fairway, almost at their maximum driving distance. The player often has ambitious expectations of being able to pass this bunker and therefore aims far too close to the bunker for comfort. The professional golfer, on the other hand, would be far more inclined to tee up on the right of the tee and aim well down the left side of the fairway to be absolutely certain of missing the bunker. How many holes on your golf course have a well-placed, nasty bunker to the right of the fairway which catches you every now and then? And on how many of these holes do you actually aim straight down the middle of the fairway instead of aiming away to the left? In this type of situation choose a very definite target well to the side of the bunker – probably quite two or three times wider than you presently aim – then set yourself up on this new target and hit purposefully towards it. Don't allow any thoughts of the ball drifting away to the right to enter your mind. *Remember that a mental picture of what you are trying to avoid can act as a set of instructions upon which your muscles react.* Instead create a vivid mental picture of a bull's-eye or white post as your driving target, focusing your attention on that and obliterating all thoughts of trouble.

Gambling and risk-taking

Gambling in its various forms is undoubtedly related to individual personality. Some people are compulsive gamblers; other people have no interest whatsoever in gambling. Some would risk everything they have on a horse; others with vast fortunes would never have a bet and prefer to tie up all their money in totally safe investments. Some people take enormous risks in their jobs or driving cars. Others see gambling as a systematic working out of the odds and a complex mathematical system of evaluating probability.

A certain type of personality is attracted far more to thoughts of success and is relatively undaunted by fear of failure; a contrasting personality is motivated not so much by

Be prepared to aim well away from the centre of the fairway to keep away from potential trouble. Tee up on the same side as the trouble and you will find it easier to aim away from it. Choose a definite spot of safety and aim positively towards it

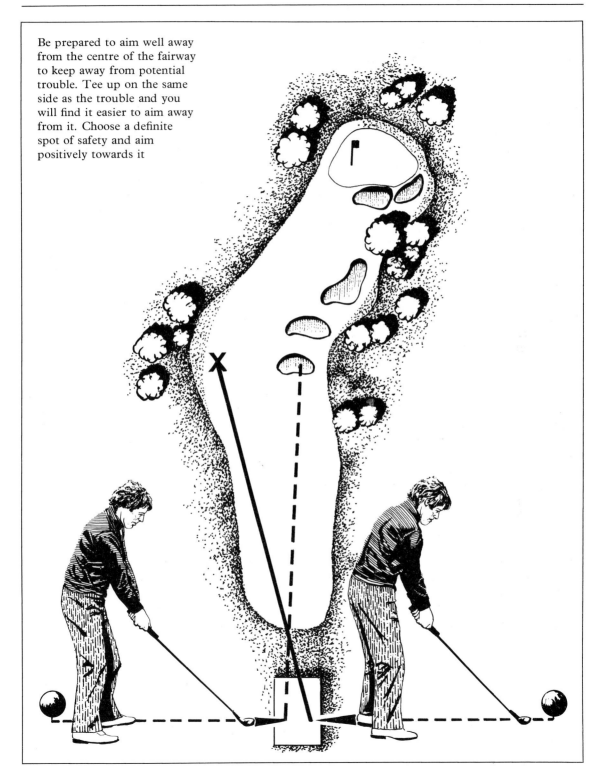

thoughts of success and winning but rather by fear of failing. It is useful to appreciate just what kind of character you are as far as your own golf is concerned. Are you the sort of person who goes out in a tournament not so much with thoughts of winning and success but rather with hopes of not doing badly and making an idiot of yourself? In many ways the person who is tremendously motivated by winning is often the person who cracks under pressure at the last moment. The desire to win may become so strong that he cannot give of his best under the pressure of success. By contrast the person who is motivated by fear of failure may often allow a bad round to become an even worse round by enveloping himself with pressure, but may, on the other hand, bring off victories when the chance is there because success doesn't mean quite so much. If he finds he is winning he may be so relieved not to be doing badly that success itself is relatively unimportant. In some ways the first type of player is far more likely to be a good match player than the second type. He may be the kind of player who produces brilliant performances one week and flops the next. The other type of character is likely to be the one who produces steadier performances and perhaps scores better in stroke play.

The type of personality and motivating instinct can also be seen in the way in which we approach different shots. It is inevitable that everybody encounters difficulties on the golf course somewhere along the line. Some players like Arnold Palmer or Seve Ballesteros often approach recovery shots in what can only be described as a reckless manner. They try for what looks to be absolutely impossible but have the skill to produce remarkable success. If they fail, they simply shrug their shoulders and have another go. A more conservative type of player will usually think out the odds of what he is doing in a more calculated way.

If you are the type of player who loves a challenge, then your type of approach to recovery and risk-taking on the golf course is likely to be relatively illogical yet exciting. For you, the whole game of golf may be centred around the fun of having a go over an extra-long carry or round a dogleg, but if this is your kind

of nature then you have to learn to live with the problems that may arise. Certainly in match play this kind of approach may be more satisfactory than in medal play.

No shot counts as half

Many golfers fail to sum up logically the situation in which they find themselves. The essence of gambling and risk-taking on the golf course is to appreciate that no shot counts as a half. Logically, if you are in a position from where it is going to take you two shots to reach the green, then those two shots count exactly the same whether you chip out with a 7 iron and hit a 4 iron to the green or manage to hit a full 9 iron from the trouble and a fifty- or sixty-yard pitch into the green. Of course, for most people there is a certain extra sense of security the closer they get to the green. But in many ways the extra risks involved in trying to obtain distance are not worth taking.

In the same way, if you are faced with the type of hole that will take you three shots to the green, then those three shots will count exactly the same whether you choose to hit a 2 wood, a 4 iron and a 6 iron, or a driver, a 4 wood and a 9 iron. The first selection of shots may leave you a simple, logical route to the green, while the second choice flirts with all sorts of difficulties and dangers, with the minor benefit of hitting three clubs less into the green. The professional golfer who is a seasoned campaigner and a sound stroke play opponent usually develops a shrewd golfing brain which enables him to assess the kind of situation and weigh up the pros and cons in a calculating manner. Two professional golfers will not necessarily approach a particular hole in the same way, but both think out very clearly the route that lies before them.

In a gambling situation remember that no shot counts as half. Two shots count the same, whether you use a driver and a 7 iron or a 3 iron and a 4 iron.

No shot counts as a half. This is a typical situation where the player is almost certainly out of range of the green. There is really no point in gambling. The risky route requires two shots to the green; the safe route requires two. The risky route may require a 7 iron followed by a short pitch; the safe route a short pitch followed by a 9 iron. The extra risk in trying to gain a little distance just isn't worthwhile

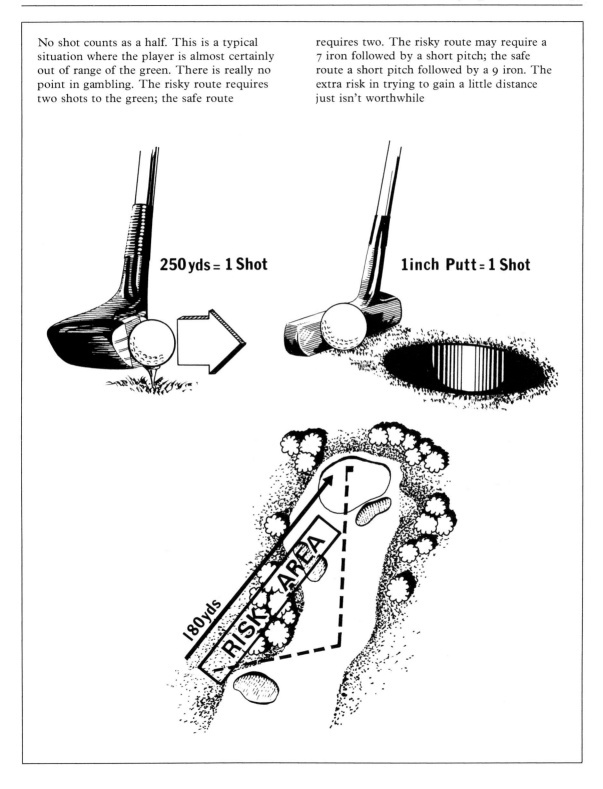

250 yds = 1 Shot

1inch Putt = 1 Shot

180 yds

RISK AREA

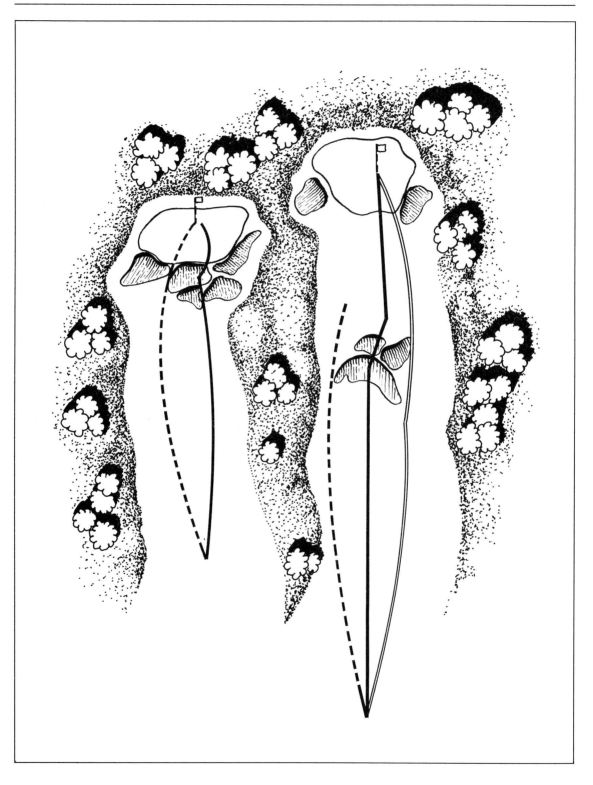

The art of gambling

One of the most common risk-taking predicaments on the golf course is a ditch or row of bunkers across the fairway. If the bunkers are very close to the green, perhaps ten yards away, and you do have a real chance of reaching the green, the gamble is probably worth taking. Providing you are a reasonably competent bunker player, the shot you would face if you did go in the bunkers would probably be no more difficult than the one you would face if you decided not to take the gamble and to play short. If the gamble succeeds, you are on the green in one; if the gamble fails, you are on the green in two; if the gamble is not taken, again you are on the green in two.

Now, supposing the bunkers are, say, fifty yards short of the green, if you just get over the bunkers are you actually going to be on the green? If not, it is quite probably a bad risk to take. If you don't get over the bunkers you may find yourself unable to get on with the next shot. Again this will depend on the type of bunker that is in the way. If you take the risk and go for the carry, you are probably going to be on in two shots and if you elected to play up short and chose the right club you would clearly have only a very short pitch into the green. But if you decided to have a go for the carry and didn't make it you would probably only be on the green in three shots. So, in other words, in this situation there is really nothing to gain from having a go at the carry. Only gamble if you do have something to gain. That is, unless you

happen to be the type of person who simply loves the thrills and spills of having a go, in which case you must take the consequences for your own indulgence!

Assessing this kind of situation in a relatively cool, calculated manner is all part of thinking your way round the golf course successfully. Distance is again a key factor in risk-taking. Possibly the most common error made by the long-handicap golfer is to decide to play short of a target and then to play far too short so that he leaves himself forty or fifty yards rather than fifteen or twenty yards short of the hazard. I would suggest to all club golfers who face this kind of decision on their own golf course that they choose a definite take-off point for gambling with the carry. Isolate, for example, one particular tree and say to yourself, 'Right, if I get to that tree I have a go and if I don't reach the tree I play short.' The only variation from this should be an allowance for having the wind either behind or against.

The reader who doesn't set out to be a swashbuckling hero on the golf course but would rather take a more sensible, if dull, approach to the game, needs to acquire a shrewd, tactical type of summing-up process for any potential occasion for risk-taking. The chief rules are perhaps these. First, take a reasonable gamble if you stand to reduce the number of shots you will actually take to reach the green. Second, don't gamble if you are simply making up distance without really reducing the difficulty of the next shot facing you. Third, ask yourself in any risk-taking situation if you stand to gain anything at all. If the answer is really no, then the gamble isn't even one worth contemplating.

The art of recovery

Playing good, consistent golf not only requires that the player should hit a very high percentage of sound golf shots; it also requires that he is able to extricate himself from trouble as efficiently as possible. Recovery shots are not in the main particularly difficult shots to execute. What the good golfer does, however, is to think

The player often faces a specific decision whether or not to attempt to carry over cross bunkers. The left-hand drawing shows a gamble which is probably worth taking. If the player fails to make the carry he can almost certainly expect to get out of the bunker and onto the green for two and is no worse off than playing short. In the other situation it is going to take two to reach the green whether he takes the risky dotted route (and succeeds) or the safe route short. If he fails to make the carry he can't reach the green in two. Realistically he gains nothing at all from the gamble, except the possibility of a slightly shorter shot to the green

logically about his approach to getting himself back into play. He sums up the situation, gauges the likelihood of success with any particular shot, considers carefully the position he would like to be in for his next shot and then plays the shot single-mindedly and with the definite purpose of playing for a specific target.

As a rule the top-class golfer is relatively unbothered by getting into trouble on the golf course and takes it very much in his stride. The club golfer, by contrast, often panics unnecessarily when he is in difficulty and tries to be far too ambitious in his choice of recovery shots. The club golfer usually tries to make up far too much ground, often taking a dangerous route across other areas of trouble, usually in the vain hope of trying to make up for his error by producing something spectacular. Many inexperienced golfers go from one trouble area to another, either because they fail to think out the shot logically or because they are unrealistic about their capabilities. Faced with the same situation, one would often find a club golfer being far more ambitious with the shot than the world-class professional. Perhaps to some extent this is because the professional golfer has greater faith in his own game and can therefore be more philosophical about playing out sideways and losing a shot, always having the hopes – if he thinks ahead – that a string of birdies may be just around the corner. The club golfer perhaps lives in constant fear of something even worse facing him in the holes to come and therefore frantically struggles to be as ambitious as possible on every shot.

In many ways the best piece of advice for making a recovery is to take the shortest possible route back to the middle of the fairway. In many situations club golfers attempt to play a particularly difficult shot in the hopes of finishing up perhaps fifty yards closer to the green than they would with a totally safe shot. If this fifty yards' potential gain only means the difference between hitting a 5 iron and hitting a pitching wedge into the green, then it may well be advisable not to attempt to make up the length and thereby risk further problems. On the other hand, if the attempt means the difference between reaching the green with the next shot and not being able to reach the green, then this

approach may be a sound one. What is essential for recovery is that the player at least thinks of his real probabilities of success and sums up the situation accurately before deciding on the route to safety.

The professional golfer is clearly more able than most club golfers to position the ball exactly where he wants. He will frequently play a well-bunkered hole by purposely zigzagging along the fairway, positioning himself in the safety areas and keeping away from the trouble zones. *Many long-handicap golfers find it almost impossible to aim in any direction except straight at the flag.* The relative beginner is often most reluctant to play a shot at a slight angle, often failing to see the potential of playing a safety shot into the correct position. This may partly be because he has relatively little confidence in being able to play the ball to an exact spot. In any potentially difficult semi-recovery situation it is essential to bear in mind the possible need to play a shot out at an angle. Where this is necessary it is vital, as in all golf shots, to choose a really specific target to aim at. Club golfers frequently play a recovery shot into a general area rather than pinpointing the exact spot they hope to hit. If you are playing out on to the fairway, learn to pick upon a really green patch of grass from where you would like to hit the next shot. Focus your mind on that position and concentrate wholeheartedly on hitting the ball there. Don't allow your mind to wander to the points of trouble you are trying to avoid. Again go back to the principle of positive thinking and positive imagery and remember that, if you allow your thoughts to focus on the things you want to avoid, these thoughts may act as instructions for your brain, tuning your body into playing towards the trouble you want to avoid just like a magnet.

Good recovery play requires a sound, logical approach to summing up the situation, together with a realistic assessment of your own capabil-

The best piece of advice in recovery situations is often to take the shortest route back to safety. Club golfers often find it difficult to turn sideways and aim away from the flag. Here we see Tony Jacklin playing out of a bunker backwards during the British Open

ities. Extremely bad scores on any hole where the player goes from one bit of trouble to another almost always result from being over-ambitious about the plan of attack and best route to safety.

Beating bad weather

Playing in bad weather can cause all sorts of problems, but on the other hand it provides a delightful challenge. For some, the biggest thrill in the game is to master a great seaside course in wind and rain that most of us would avoid at all costs. Windy conditions require the most solid of techniques and respect (but not fear) for the difficulties. Whenever you are playing into a cross-wind, it is important to decide whether you are going to allow for the wind by aiming away to the side of the target or whether you are going to try to fade or draw the fall to combat the wind. Some players prefer the first approach and others the second. This really depends largely on your ability to draw or fade the ball at will and on whether you do have one predominantly curved shot which can be used to advantage in windy conditions. The key point once again is to be absolutely certain of the approach you are taking and not to be caught between two ideas, or the shot will be destined for failure. If you do decide to aim off to one side or the other, then do bear in mind that most people allow too little for a cross-wind and also tend to forget that the ball is likely to bounce away to the side as it lands on the green. It is essential to choose a definite target, picking out a tree or a bunker in the distance, and to aim methodically at this rather than having some vague hope of just hitting away to the side of the green. The more definite you can be in your own mind, the more likely you are to succeed.

Hitting the ball downwind causes relatively few problems for the club golfer. A tailwind can be a great advantage, not only in the added length it helps to produce but also because it will tend to straighten out a curving shot. What is essential in playing downwind is to get the ball well up into the air – bearing in mind that a tailwind can in fact reduce the height produced. With a tee shot you may find it helpful to hit the ball with a 3 wood instead of the driver or may find that teeing the ball slightly higher and concentrating on nipping the tee peg as you strike the ball helps to create added loft.

What is more likely to be a problem when playing downwind is hitting the shots into the green. This is particularly true of the top-class player who is seeking to get the ball really close to the hole. In many ways playing downwind requires considerable courage and it is often quite a daunting task for the professional golfer to maintain the bravado to fly the ball right into the green. The temptation is often to land the ball too far short of the flag. Instead of catching a reasonably well-watered green, the ball all too often lands on the hard part of the fairway and shoots through the green; this understandably leads to an increasingly timid approach. Playing downwind requires a bold approach to shots, often aiming the ball right into the heart of the green where there is maximum chance of it stopping. Here again, good planning of the golf course and sound knowledge of the problem areas can be of assistance. *The more accurate your knowledge of what is behind the green and the exact distances involved, the easier it is to play a bold attacking shot.*

Playing into the wind is probably the most difficult task for all but the very skilled player. A strong headwind not only obviously takes off distance in the flight of the ball but also tends to exaggerate the height. The higher-handicap golfer can take a certain amount of encouragement from a headwind by having added confidence in the fairway woods and long irons, secure in the knowledge that the headwind will, if anything, help the ball into the air. The great art of playing into a strong wind is to be prepared to take plenty of club and *not* to try to hit the ball harder – if anything, to try to play the shot with a slower, smoother and more balanced swing. Most golfers tend to underclub into the wind and therefore hit the ball far harder than usual. Attacking the ball with extra vigour in this way often adds to the backspin that is produced, floating the ball higher into the

Playing into the wind requires good knowledge of distance and of the problems, if any, behind the green. This enables the player to take plenty of club and to concentrate on a slow, smooth swing, maintaining perfect balance. The club golfer tends to underclub, forcing the swing, which puts added backswing and height onto the shots. Don't fight the wind. Just take plenty of club

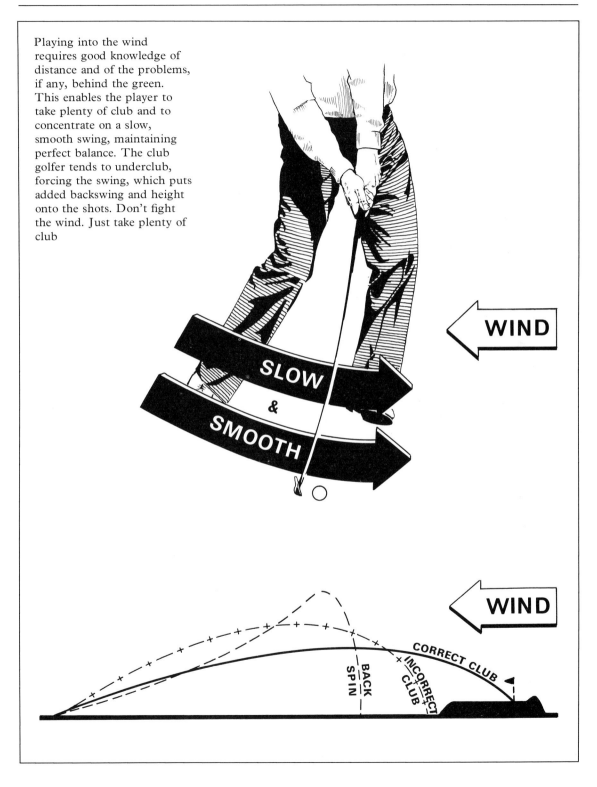

air and producing erratic direction *The philosophy of playing into the wind is* not *to fight the wind but simply to take masses of extra club, swinging smoothly and concentrating on perfect balance.* The really top-class player can always be seen to maintain perfect tempo in the wind and will usually produce an absolutely firm, solid followthrough without any tendency to lose control. On the other hand, the less expert golfer can almost always be seen to be fighting the wind and thus losing control.

Here again, it is essential to have as good a knowledge of the distances on the golf course as possible. If, for example, you are faced with a shot of 150 yards into a strong headwind, you may well need mentally to add 30 yards on to this to assess the correct clubbing. If your knowledge of the course also tells you that you have a further 20 yards' margin beyond the flag before you are faced with any problems, you can rely on having 200 yards to work with. This may well encourage you to take sufficient club; without this additional information it is hard to be bold enough. Bear in mind that hitting a ball into the wind requires an exceptionally well-struck shot in order to hold the ball's direction. Any tendency to draw or fade the ball will be exaggerated into the wind and perfect direction will therefore be lost. Again, the smoother and more controlled the swing, the better the chance of holding the line with the shot. Take plenty of club and don't fight the wind.

Wet weather blues

Rainy conditions bring out the worst in some players and the best in others. A dull, overcast day with the rain lashing down often brings an atmosphere of gloom and despondency to the whole game, many players finding it difficult to keep up their morale in order to continue battling on. It is all too easy to have a self-pitying approach, feeling demoralized and thoroughly dejected about the weather and any bad shots that follow. One of the most useful measures to counteract bad weather is again to think of every shot as an isolated unit, just concentrating on playing that particular stroke to the best of your ability. In this way any overall dejection can very often be avoided and morale kept as high as possible.

In rainy conditions the obvious problem is how to keep yourself dry, keep the grips on the clubs dry *and concentrate.* One of the usual reasons why players find rainy conditions difficult is that their attention tends to wander, and they spend far more time thinking of the rain and how wet everything is getting than concentrating on getting on with the job. The warmer and more muffled up you are and the drier you can keep yourself and your equipment, the brighter your outlook is bound to be. Some good players maintain that you should always have a really brightly coloured set of rainwear and a colourful umbrella to bring a ray of sunshine to a wet day and provide a cheerful influence! Perhaps there is something in this, because certainly the less you moan about the weather and the more cheerful you can be the more likely your attitude towards the game is to remain positive.

The great thing about playing in any sort of adverse weather conditions is to see it as just another challenge of the game and not to allow yourself to give up in despair. Try to see it as a separate game, thinking as methodically about the weather conditions and the extra problems as you do about the rest of your game. Remember that if it is raining on you it is raining on your opponents. See the game as a test for your good humour and you may well find that learning to enjoy the challenge improves your performance.

Keys for straighter driving

Although the old cliché is that one drives for show and putts for dough, driving is certainly one of the most important parts of the game and is often a key to a good score. The player who can reliably hit every fairway from the tee is almost always en route to a good score.

As far as technique in driving is concerned, the basic principle is to play the ball well forward in the feet, producing a shallow takeaway and shallow attack on the ball where the bottom of the swing is perhaps eight or ten inches behind the ball. In this way the ball is struck slightly on the upswing for maximum length and carry. This combined with sound balance and a positive mental approach should set the player up for a successful score. Of course, any fault in technique with the other clubs is exaggerated with the driver. The lack of loft with the driver means that the clubhead strikes the ball very near to its equator and therefore tends to put on less backspin and more sidespin than with any of the other clubs. Any tendency to hook or slice the ball will show up with the driver far more than it will with any other club. To a certain extent there is therefore no hope of driving really well unless the overall grip and technique are relatively sound.

For many golfers, however, the failing of their driving is not so much one of technique as one of having a poor mental attitude. Good driving requires a really positive attack on the ball and a positive mental approach. It is essential to choose a definite target to aim at, a specific tree or spot on the horizon, not some vague general aiming area. If the likely landing area is visible, choose a target for distance, not just direction. This helps to curb any tendency to thrash the ball too hard towards a target on the horizon. The target down the fairway must be absolutely definite, whether the fairway is narrow and tree-lined or whether it is wide open and comparatively trouble free. Once you have chosen a definite target and aimed at this, it is essential to hit the ball at the same kind of strength to every drive. There is absolutely no point in trying to steer the ball down the fairway on one shot and trying to blast it out of the county on the next. The speed of the swing and overall balance and control must stay as constant as possible from the start of the round to the finish. For many golfers the problem with driving is that they are so lacking in confidence that instead of making a positive swing at the ball they try to nudge it away down the fairway with a halfhearted attack. Consequently the clubhead slows down before it strikes the ball and will exaggerate any tendency to hook or slice. Golfers frequently take a good, free practice swing on the tee and then tighten up drastically in their swing with the ball. In this

way the clubhead speed is lost and the end of the swing is usually short and stunted. The swing with the ball must be as full and free as the practice swing and must continue right on through to a really solid, majestic followthrough, with good legwork and perfect balance.

The soundest piece of advice for all golfers, of every standard, is to adopt a method with driving which has perfect balance and enables the player to hold the finish of the swing for a count of at least three or four seconds. *The best practice technique for any aspiring golfer is to learn to hit full-blooded drives, holding the end of the swing until the ball has actually landed.* This means that the swing must be kept in perfect control so that there is no question of losing stability through impact. Most golfers allow their finish to become shorter and shorter under pressure, and one often sees potentially good young professionals or top amateurs failing to give of their best by producing a scrappy swing in competition. The world-class golfer will be seen to swing the same from the start to the end of the tournament, producing a swing that is perfectly balanced and methodical.

For good driving, again it is essential to have a clear, positive image of what you are trying to accomplish and never to allow a negative mental image to enter the mind. Remember that thoughts of trying *not* to slice or hook the ball will produce a picture which acts as a mental set of instructions to the body, making the hook or slice all the more likely.

Concepts for driving

There are several concepts which may be of assistance in hitting the ball well from the tee. The first is to imagine a large target hanging down in front of you perhaps twenty yards ahead and on line with the middle of the fairway. Concentrate on having the feeling of banging the ball into this huge target; if you are able to start the ball absolutely straight for the first twenty yards you will almost always find that a straight drive will follow. A positive mental target like this can help eliminate any thoughts of the trouble down the fairway.

Another approach is to imagine a huge open umbrella positioned in the middle of the fairway to catch the ball. Try to imagine the ball sailing through the air and plopping into it. Again, creating a mental picture like this tends to block out any negative thoughts of the trouble around and gives a good reliable picture which can be conjured up in any playing situation. Another excellent concept is to think of a huge wall about twenty yards in front of you with a large hole through which you have to drive the ball. Again this tends to focus the mind on the correct path of the shot and blots out anything else around. Some such kind of concept can be taken out into every situation and provides a mental routine which will overcome troublesome drives.

For the person whose technique is good enough, sound driving is a question of choosing a target, eliminating fear and inhibitions, and taking a nice free swing at the ball to send it on its way. The player who produces a bad drive at certain narrow or tree-lined holes usually falls into the trap of trying to steer the ball down the middle of the fairway instead of having the necessary freedom. My own philosophy of driving is that if I am going to be unlucky enough – *and note I say 'unlucky'* – to have my ball go in the trees I might as well relax and enjoy it and at least hit the ball as far as possible. Think of the shot as being 'unlucky' – a question of probability – and relieve yourself of the burden of blame. If you are a good golfer who produces the odd bad drive, try to resist the feeling that *you* did it or that *you* made it go there. If you allow yourself to think in this way, you will tend to put pressure on yourself, castigating your own faults, and probably resulting in your doing exactly the same thing on another hole. If, by contrast, you can become relatively detached from the shot, putting the shot down to pure bad luck and something quite

out of your control, then you should find yourself far less inhibited about other drives.

Stand up, let rip and remember that the ball is sitting on the ground in front of you just longing to fly through the air to the other end of the 'elastic'. The only way it can't go straight is if you steer it or prod it. Find freedom and release the ball to set it on its way. If you are going to hit a bad shot, well at least take a free swing at it and enjoy yourself. In a potentially stressful situation on the golf course, try to imagine that the ball can only fly back to the other end of its elastic; it doesn't matter what you do, providing you have perfect freedom and release the ball from where it is sitting.

Although looseness and freedom are essential, it is important to realize that you can only hit the ball a certain length from the tee and that there is very little point in trying to strive for additional distance. It is awfully tempting when playing with someone who hits the ball further than you do to try to hit the ball harder in an attempt to keep up. *You will in fact find that trying to hit the ball extra distance in this way usually results in a forced kind of swing which actually reduces clubhead speed and often results in a shorter shot being produced.* There is no point whatsoever in attempting to hit the ball especially hard. Live with the distance you can produce and try to keep the overall speed of attack on the ball as constant as possible from one hole to the next and from one game to the next.

First-tee nerves

Most golfers loathe going off the first tee. Whether they are top tournament professionals or amateur golfers, almost everyone finds the first-tee shot a nasty experience. Why should it be? For many people it is the first shot of the day; they probably haven't been on the practice ground and loosened up with a few shots. They may walk on to the first tee wondering or worrying about their standard for the day. Then again, the shot may cause problems because you feel that people who watch you go from the first tee may never see you hit another shot and may

Good balance is essential for straight consistent driving. Adopt a method in which you definitely retain balance at the end of the swing for a good three or four seconds. Under pressure this may reduce slightly but you will still find yourself under perfect control. Practise hitting full-blooded drives and holding the finish until the ball touches down

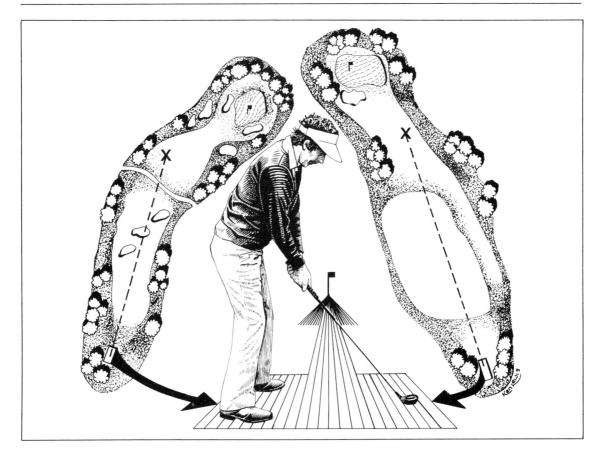

Seve Ballesteros showing the freedom and looseness necessary for good driving, with a full, balanced finish

judge your whole performance on what they see of that one drive. To a certain extent that is true. In addition you may simply not like having people watching and the first tee may be a particularly public place.

Perhaps the most comforting thought for the club golfer is that the majority of top professionals hate playing off the first tee just as much as the club golfer does. Every golfer has sympathy for every other golfer playing that first-tee shot. So how do you combat first-tee nerves?

For the club golfer the basic rule is this. Have a few practice swings before you get on to the tee and then when you do tee up the ball concentrate on two things: on watching the ball but then also on producing the best-*looking* swing you possibly can. Imagine that you are swinging through to a majestic finish, with perfect bal-

Left: If confronted with a difficult tee shot, imagine that you are on a tee at your home course, where your thoughts are positive and you feel confident of hitting a good shot, instead of worrying about the hazards facing you. Any drive is simply a question of standing on a flat square of ground with the ball on a tee peg and hitting it to the target you choose down the fairway

ance and a followthrough that you can hold two or three seconds in case there is someone there taking a photograph! If you make a good-looking swing with perfect balance, not only will it bring out the best in your technique and give you every chance of hitting the ball well, but in addition, even if you don't hit the ball well, everyone will at least think you are a good golfer on an off day. Amazingly enough, if you finish the swing with a really good, poised, majestic followthrough, holding your finish and looking straight down the fairway, most people will probably assume you have hit a good shot and quite probably won't even notice where the ball goes. This way you can fool most of the people most of the time!

For the experienced golfer the main rule is to loosen up and relax as much as possible before playing. If tension is likely to creep in anywhere during the round of golf, it will probably be on the first or last tee. Again, don't fall into the trap of trying to *make* yourself hit a good drive down the first hole. Try to take the view of *allowing* it to happen and being as free and loose as you possibly can. If you do feel nervous on the first tee, analyse why this is so. If it really boils down to wanting to do well in front of a gallery who may not see any other shot, then concentrate on

exactly the same thing as the club golfer. In other words, try to make the swing *look* absolutely perfect. Make the finish of the swing majestic, maintain perfect balance, and the overall effect will be impressive, even if the shot is less than perfect.

If you have perfect control over your mental resources, why not try to forget you are on the first tee. Try to imagine you are still on the practice tee, or that you have played a few holes and, if you like, are simply setting off down the seventh or eighth hole, or whatever, with a perfectly routine drive. It is a question of analysing your inner fears and failings and then using some mental trick to overcome them – perhaps an illusion regarding the time and place, or the illusion of posing for the photographer.

Make it look good and the result will be success – or, at worst, the illusion of success!

10 Scoring: Forgetting Past and Future

The third stage in mastering the game is the ability to score well round the golf course. To many golfers, both amateur and professional, it comes as something of a shock to realize that this skill can be quite separate from and un-related to mastery of both swing and shotmak-ing. Some golfers score far better than the outward appearance of their swing and striking would suggest; others display technical perfec-tion and superficial genius while the scoring ability eludes them.

The art of scoring is found not in technique, nor solely in experience, but in the golfing mind. In many instances the relatively unthink-ing golfer may have certain advantages over his more intellectual counterpart. What he may lack in the acquired knowledge and wisdom of strategic planning may be offset by a calmness and stillness of mind which is perhaps less destructive and less distracted by thoughts of past and future. The player who performs in this way is likely to suffer from bad planning, lack of desire and weaknesses of technique which accompany lack of curiosity. The player with a particularly lively, inquiring mind has the advantages of his experience in so far as strategy and technique are concerned, but for him the problem is one of quieting and empty-ing the mind of past memories and doubts about the future. The art of scoring is very much a question of focusing the concentration, ridding the mind of superfluous thought and working on practised principles of mental control.

Central to the game of scoring are the prob-lems of the stationary ball and of 'living in the past and future'. The more lively your mind, the more potentially destructive the problems.

As we have seen previously, the problem of the stationary ball is not a physical but a mental one. The reflex reactions and fast-speed judgements that are used with a moving ball tend to be lost with a stationary one because the player has too much time for analysis. In order to score well the player must go through a process of intro-spection, comparing his practice/play thinking and weighing up when and how destructive thoughts are allowed to creep in. The art of scoring is a question of thinking sufficiently hard in order to assess the situation through past-acquired wisdom, while thinking suffic-iently little to avoid being destructive. Perfect-ing the golfing mind is a question of balancing the two.

Living in the past and future

The sixth problem for the golfing mind is one of keeping the mind functioning firmly in the present. This difficulty follows on from the stationary ball problem, the mind having far too much time to wander away into past and future, becoming sidetracked and confused, and producing doubts and indecision.

When you think of the past you are likely to think of previous experiences with this kind of shot, not usually benefiting from prior mistakes but rather allowing doubts and indecision to occur. You may look back with regret at the last shot or previous holes, blaming yourself for being in a certain position or in some way pressurizing yourself to make up for previous errors. You may give yourself time to look to the future. What if I hit the ball too hard? What if I don't keep far enough left? What happens if I don't make my par? I hope I don't fluff the shot. The extra seconds which the mind has in striking a stationary ball rather than a moving ball can lead the golfing mind to be at its most destructive.

In order to counter this problem, you must keep your mind firmly positioned in the present. Never look backwards in time. Never, except for planning your position, look forward in time. Learn to limit your thoughts to perception of the present time and you are well on the road to finding the elusive art of scoring.

A personal revelation

I am certain that the greatest transformation in my own game of golf, both as player and as teacher, came about through realizing one particular point that I have already mentioned: a game of golf is made up of a number of totally separate shots. I began to appreciate that producing a good score was simply a matter of stringing together as many good shots and as few bad shots as possible. But what I also realized was that I and almost every other golfer, both amateur and professional, viewed these shots as being linked in some way, so that one shot was allowed to affect another. I began to look at my own golf more critically and saw that my mental approach to shots varied quite unnecessarily. I could see, for example, that I had a different attitude towards a fairway wood to the green on a short par five than towards a fairway wood on a long par four; I approached the shot in a different way if I was scoring badly than if I was leading the field. I realized that I had yet another different approach if I had perhaps driven into the trees, chipped out and was in some way trying to make up for my previous error. On closely analysing my game I found that this occurred with every type of shot. The chip or pitch where I was struggling to

make par was somehow more pressured than the one where I had a good chance of making a birdie. The four-foot putt for a two was not approached in the same way as a four-foot putt for a six.

What I immediately discovered was that this was detrimental to my game. And then I looked at others, those I watched and those I taught, and it became obvious that most of them were affected in exactly the same way as I was, the club golfer suffering unnecessary disasters and a professional like myself failing to capitalize fully from his or her own potential. And then I also began to learn that a few players possessed the gift or acquired the discipline – I'm not sure which – of being able to see each particular golf shot as an entirely separate task. I realized that this single-minded, concentrated approach enabled them to attack each shot in virtually the same way, whether winning or losing, competing or not competing, playing at home or abroad, struggling for a bogey or hoping for an eagle. In fact I discovered that when taken to extremes they no longer struggled for bogeys or hoped for eagles but simply concentrated on each shot in a totally detached manner.

With this realization I became determined not only to learn this ability myself but to indoctrinate my pupils with the same discipline. Learning this 'single-shot technique' was by no means easy. Even now, I suppose I catch myself with the odd stray thought but invariably bring my attention back on track. But the very day I started trying to learn the technique my golf improved. I began to be able to look at shots in a far more detached and rational way. I would think to myself, 'Here I am trying to hit this ball from A to B with a 5 iron.' My concentration improved, I began to be able to ignore what had gone before, how I was scoring, and so on. Having played that shot I would then forget about it, whether good or bad, as quickly as possible and walk to wherever the ball might be, approaching the next shot in exactly the same uncomplicated way. I began to lose the disastrous urge to try to make up for previous errors or thinking of what lay ahead. I found a game of golf far less mentally strenuous – I suppose because my concentration became centred around each shot, thus casting out unnecessary and presumably burdensome thoughts.

My mental approach to golf changed dramatically. By seeing the game as being purely and simply made up of a number of single, self-contained shots I was beginning to manage not only to approach each shot with the same mental attitude but to cast errors out of my mind with far greater ease. Since I no longer dwelt on bad shots, they were no longer allowed to affect me. I began to play a totally new mental game on the course, which not only made each game become much more satisfying but also made me a better golfer. My new mental approach required me to play each shot to the best of my ability regardless of the score, the nature of the competition, the opposition, and so on. I would think to myself, 'Supposing I was just demonstrating this in a clinic, talking through the shot with my audience.' What in turn followed from this was that my own satisfaction from each shot came not only from how close the ball landed to the hole but also from pleasure at my own composure and undistracted thoughts. In this way the external performance became almost less important than the internal one. In some ways I derived greater satisfaction from perfect mental control of the game than I did from the actual score. I realized that with perfecting this technique I would virtually conquer the mental game of golf.

Almost every golfer, whether amateur or professional, falls into the trap of seeing shots as being linked together so that one shot is allowed to affect another. Except among those who are exceptionally well disciplined in the way I have described above, the golfer will invariably try to make up for what has gone before, either trying to recover from a poor shot by taking unjustifiable risks or by pressurizing himself to make a birdie to recover from a dropped shot. The disciplined training you must have is to see the game of golf as made up of a number of totally separate shots, so that the mind is simply focused for any particular shot on playing that shot to the best of your ability. The object is simply to strike the ball from A to B. There is no question of trying to make up for what has gone before or of compensating for errors.

Stroke play techniques

Most professional golfers generally prefer stroke play tournaments to match play ones. Stroke play is generally considered to be a better test because it is more exacting. Every shot in the game counts, there is no question of bad holes being recorded as just a relatively insignificant loss, and the score at the end of the day is plain for all to see. Club golfers often prefer match play because at the end of the round they can kid themselves that their overall score was really much better than it was. In stroke play the card never lies and you have only yourself to blame or to praise for results. In match play there is always the excuse that the opponent played particularly well – a sort of psychological let-out for a bad result. In stroke play there are no excuses.

The essence of good stroke play is to realize that the round is made up of so many isolated shots. The person who plays stroke play well will usually be able to treat each shot as a separate unit, forgetting very much about the overall score and simply thinking of producing the best possible result with every shot. Many club golfers find stroke play difficult because their mind is always going back to previous errors as well as forward to the overall score being built up. Club golfers will often be very conscious of how many over par they are, whether they are performing better or worse than their handicap level, and so on. This tends to influence the way in which they play their next shot, and they often attempt to make up for previous errors or play cautiously in order not to spoil previous successes. This is really quite the wrong way of approaching stroke play.

The correct approach to stroke play is to start on the first tee by trying to produce the best possible drive you can; from wherever that lands, trying to produce the best possible second shot you can; from there, putting to the best of your ability, and so on. *The frequent mistake which all but top-class players make is to try to compensate for their errors.* A typical example of this would be where a player has driven into the trees on a par five, chipped on to the fairway for two and is then faced with an exceptionally difficult third shot to the green. He may have no real prospect of reaching the green without flirting with all sorts of hazards on the way. Had he driven into the present position instead of being there for two his approach would quite probably be to play a safe shot with a 4 wood or long iron, hoping from there to pitch into the green and, if thinking ahead, of obtaining his birdie in this way. The error he quite probably makes now is to try to make up for his wayward drive by taking out his 2 wood, playing a shot that is far too risky, in the hopes of making the green in three, and thereby quite probably finishing up with a bogey or real disaster. The lesson to learn is that from this particular position on the fairway the approach to the next shot should be exactly the same whether you have driven there for one, chipped out of the trees for two or have even had to hit three off the tee.

There is no question in stroke play of ever compensating for what has gone before. All you should be trying to do is to play every shot to the best of your ability. An error made is a shot lost and you cannot make up for it. Live firmly in the present.

An equally important point to appreciate about stroke play is that a round of golf can be made up in many ways. You may start a round by dropping seven shots on the first three holes and be four under for the next fifteen. Equally you may be four under par for the first fifteen

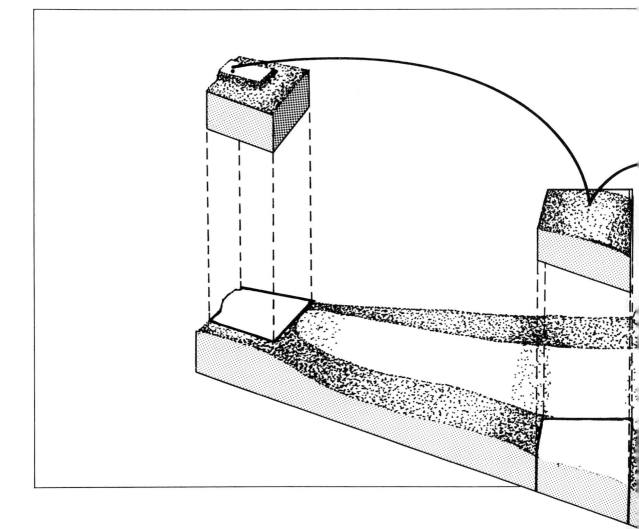

holes and seven over for the last three. The result at the end of the round is exactly the same. But it will be the same only if you can cast out of your mind previous errors and simply plod on in the hopes of playing every shot perfectly. Most golfers who start the round badly become so demoralized that they never recover their composure and simply go from bad to worse. The person who is a trained stroke play player will usually be able to cast aside thoughts of any such errors, appreciating that three bad holes on a round can just as easily come in sequence at the beginning as at the end of the round, or that the three bad holes may be spaced fairly evenly throughout the round. In many ways this realization comes only with

experience and there is no better such experience for an aspiring golfer than to have a round of golf made up of a disastrous start or even a disastrous front nine, followed by a spectacular finish. This does wonders for encouraging the player in all future situations to ignore both past and future or to believe that a spectacular finish is quite likely to occur.

The philosophy of probability

Perhaps the most helpful approach to overcoming errors in stroke play is to consider that the game of golf is very largely a question of probability. At a certain level the probability is that you will hit, say, 80 per cent of drives on to

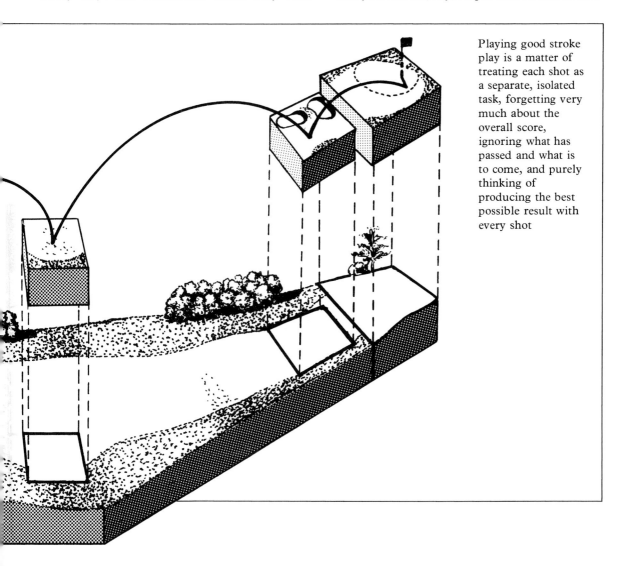

Playing good stroke play is a matter of treating each shot as a separate, isolated task, forgetting very much about the overall score, ignoring what has passed and what is to come, and purely thinking of producing the best possible result with every shot

A frequent mistake is to try to make up for errors, playing unrealistically ambitious shots. If you hook your drive out of bounds and have to take three off the tee, don't force it in a vain attempt to make up for the past fault. Don't try for an extra long one when in reality you risk more trouble. The approach from a particular position should be identical whether you have driven there, chipped out of the trees, or taken three off the tee. You cannot make up for what has gone before

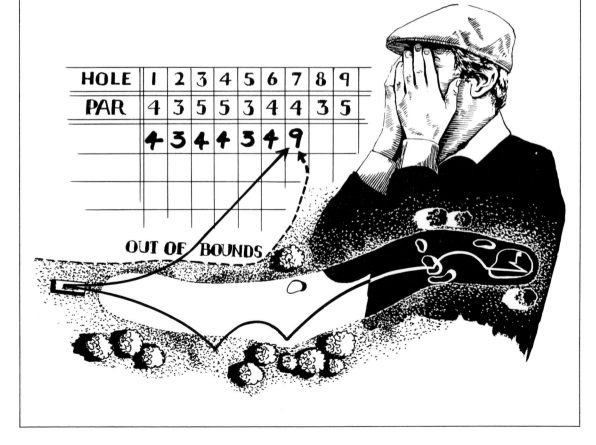

the fairway, hit 80 per cent of greens in regulation, hole 90 per cent of putts under six foot, and so on. The exact figures don't, of course, need to be very precise. But what it means is that you come to realize that certain errors will crop up from time to time in accordance with your probable level of success. This doesn't mean that you should in any way anticipate errors, but when they do arise you simply say to yourself, 'Ah, well, that's just one of my percentage of drives which hasn't hit the fairway.' If you can adopt this relatively philosophical approach to your errors, they are not likely to be compounded by additional errors, one following after the other. If you happen to miss three fairways off the tee on consecutive holes, this doesn't necessarily mean that your driving has gone to pot. It may simply mean that on average you hit about eleven fairways out of fourteen from the tee and that those three misses just happen to have followed each other. If you can look upon your errors in this way it can be very comforting. You can in a way be encouraged by the fact that an error is more likely to be followed by a success than by another error! After all, one less than perfect drive doesn't *cause* another less than perfect shot. The bad shot doesn't mean that you have lost your whole technique; it simply means that on that particular shot you didn't perform at your best level. Bad shots follow other bad shots in an unpleasant sequence only if the player allows his mental state to change, so that he becomes demoralized and fails to give of his best in the next stroke.

Monitoring motivation

Equally important in stroke play is to assess your mental attitudes during the short game and putting. Do you approach a ten-foot putt in a quite different way if the putt is for a birdie than if the putt is for a par? In fact the task is exactly the same – that is, to get the ball into the hole. Some people allow themselves to putt better when they are putting for birdies and other people putt better when they are putting for a par. To the first group, a birdie putt may in some ways cause less pressure than a putt for a

par. After all, even if the putt does miss the chances are that a par will result. On the other hand, players who putt better for a par perhaps concentrate better when they feel they are saving par; they may be slightly bolder with the putt or they may be slightly more cautious. Yet in reality both types of putts are exactly the same. You should just try to do your best and if the putt for a birdie fails this is a potentially lost shot in exactly the same way as if a putt for a par fails. If you do find yourself approaching these shots with a very different mental approach, it is important to ask yourself why you have this different outlook on the shot and to investigate exactly what produces the best possible results.

It is important for the tournament golfer to assess his own approach to a particularly good stroke play round. Do you become over-cautious at the end of a good round by trying very hard not to spoil what has gone before? Do you on the other hand become extremely tense and worried about ruining a potentially good score or are you able to carry on regardless in the correct way, simply concentrating on producing perfection with every shot and allowing the score to take care of itself? The latter is the correct approach. Don't look forward; don't look back.

Try to remember when playing the last two holes of the round that the shots facing you are exactly the same whether you happen to be four under par or fourteen over par. The hole will require a good tee shot, a good second shot, or whatever. The game requires that you give of your best for each of these individual shots. If you allow yourself to become cautious and defensive then you are changing the mental approach quite unnecessarily. A cautious approach almost always results in a halfhearted swing and a bad shot. Don't play safe just because you are doing well, unless it is simply a question of choosing a shorter club than usual and still hitting it with full authority. But, on the whole, the last two or three holes of every round should be attacked in exactly the same way, regardless of the type of score you are producing. All too often one sees tournament results where one player needed only two pars to win the tournament or perhaps even a par and a bogey, but surprisingly failed to

Remember that the shot facing you is just the same whether you are four under par or fourteen over. Don't become cautious or defensive if you are doing well, or overambitious and reckless if doing badly. Neither approach will bring out your best

do this. Almost certainly the player's attack on the closing holes has been allowed to become cautious and defensive. Instead of attacking the ball and simply trying to play each shot perfectly he probably tried to steer the ball into position, thinking too far ahead, and thus allowing an error to creep in.

Stroke play is in some ways more difficult than match play, basically because the score on the card tells all. It is a 'game of no excuses'. Once you can learn to see the round as being composed of isolated units and think only in terms of the present, then your score will improve.

Match play: the infallible foe

Although it is perhaps generally accepted that stroke play is a better test of golf and is more exacting in its requirements, many golfers find match play equally difficult for different reasons. The theory is that if you can tackle match play in exactly the same way as you tackle stroke play, concentrating on each single shot and working at producing the best possible score, this will suffice against your opponent. The difficulty, of course, is that it is so easy to be influenced by the way in which your opponent is performing. Some match play exponents say that they definitely pit their wits against the opponent rather than concentrating on the score as in a stroke play round. Others maintain that the correct approach to match play is to concentrate on the score for each hole, assuming that wins will follow. There is little doubt that, even if you do follow this second approach, the shots produced by your opponent are almost certainly going to have some influence on your own thinking.

What is of paramount importance in match play is to avoid being sidetracked into making mistakes by paying too much attention to your opponent's performance. In a typical instance in match play, player A is perhaps in the greenside bunker for three while player B is facing his second shot to the green. All too often player B assumes that a win is in the bag, relaxes with his second shot, perhaps doesn't give of his

best and finds himself finishing up with a five. Meanwhile his opponent splashes out of the bunker and down the hole. Again, the player has fallen into the trap of looking forward in time and having expectations of a win rather than living firmly in the present. In a way this produces a double change of events. Not only does player B finish up losing the hole when he expected to win it, but he is almost certainly likely to be demoralized by the result. Player A gets a tremendous psychological lift at his spectacular recovery. In stroke play there would be little mental reaction between the players. Player B would still be concentrating on making his par and if he failed and only made five the odds are he would not be particularly demoralized.

What is also most noticeable in match play is that the underdog will often become greatly elated if he is managing to keep up with his usually better opponent. This type of boost to his ego probably brings out the best in his own golf, gradually even wearing down his superior opponent who becomes frustrated at not producing the results he expects.

There is one particular trick of match play which, once mastered, at least goes part way towards avoiding that dreadful sinking feeling when an opponent is performing particularly well or does something remarkable. This is the concept of 'the infallible foe'.

The principle of 'the infallible foe' is that you must always imagine your opponent is going to produce his very best shot under all circumstances. This doesn't mean that you should in any way panic when you are playing your own shot, but that when your opponent is about to play a shot you always imagine that he will produce the perfect result. In other words, if your opponent is positioned in the greenside bunker for three and you are sitting nicely on the green for three, you have to imagine, as he sets up to take his stroke, that his shot is likely to be absolutely perfect and even go down the hole. If you can gear yourself up into believing this, it is a tremendous advantage. If your opponent produces a really successful shot then it doesn't leave you surprised or deflated in any way; that is what you have imagined is likely to happen.

The infallible foe. When your opponent is playing his shot always expect it to be successful. If he plays a perfect shot it doesn't surprise and deflate you. If he fails it gives you a tremendous boost

On the other hand, if he produces a less than perfect shot, this gives you a psychological lift – the error being totally unexpected.

Similarly, if your opponent has a twenty-foot putt for his par and you have a three-foot putt for yours, the principle of the infallible foe dictates that you imagine he is going to hole his putt. If he succeeds, you are not in any way deflated and can approach your own putt confidently. On the other hand, if he just misses with his putt this acts as a mental bonus for you and should again help you psychologically.

Once mastered, the concept of the infallible foe will set you in very good stead for match play tournaments. If you analyse your psychological approach in match play, you will probably find that the most difficult problems to overcome occur when your opponent produces something out of the ordinary. Once you can gear yourself up to watching each of his strokes in the assumption that he will produce perfection, your psychological approach to match play will be considerably strengthened.

Ignoring past and future

Another important aspect of match play is that enormous swings of fortune can take place on the golf course. It is not uncommon for one player to be five or six holes up and then to have this lead whittled away as the other player draws level. A player who has a commanding lead and suddenly finds himself losing it often suffers a severe psychological setback. Again, this type of position requires a very definite mental approach. The first lesson is that you should never slacken up your attack on the course and your opponent just because you appear to have a sizeable lead. Never feel *any* sympathy until the match is won. Remember that many good rounds are produced by a player going out in thirty-three and back in forty, but the score at the end of the day is exactly the same as the player who goes out in forty and back in thirty-three. In just the same way one player may win six of the first nine holes but the other player has every opportunity of winning six of the second nine holes. Big swings in matches can take place.

Train yourself only to think of the score – if you must think of it at all – on the particular hole you are playing. Remember that three up is three up, whether you have previously been six up or two down. The ideal approach is simply to look upon the present situation and think to yourself, for example, 'Supposing this was a five-hole match and I was told I was three up and five to go, I'd think my odds were very good. The fact that I was six up at one time is quite irrelevant.' If you must think of the score, only think of the present score, cutting out from your mind whatever has gone before.

Learn to live firmly in the present time on the golf course. Don't look back – regretting your errors or trying to make up for them. Don't look forward – anticipating success or failure, doubting your ability or worrying about the result. Learn to think of only the present, and to treat every shot as the single, isolated task it really is.

Successful scoring

1. **The single shot technique.**

2. **Accept that there are no excuses.**

3. **Think in the present – not past or future.**

4. **Never try to make up for errors – forget them.**

5. **See errors as the fate of probability.**

6. **Play with a constant level of motivation.**

7. **Your opponent is the infallible foe.**

11 The Game of No Excuses

The search for the perfect golfing mind finishes as it started with a look at our fears and inhibitions, our worries at not succeeding, our search for the excuse behind which to shelter. It returns to the other inherent difficulty of the scoring game, which is in many ways the hardest to conquer: the problem of 'the game of no excuses'.

Any game involving a stationary ball makes particular mental demands on the player. What the player does with a stationary ball is almost entirely dependent on himself; he puts the ball into play, and the success or failure of each shot is his responsibility. There are very few excuses. In moving-ball games each shot follows on and leads up to other shots, usually played by another player or players. Failure over any particular shot can often be excused as being caused by the opponent's success rather than your own poor shot. This reduces the mental pressure and allows the player to hide behind such excuses. In golf there are no excuses at all.

Indeed, golf is perhaps a unique sport in that each player plays his own ball from start to finish; everything that happens to it is his responsibility and his alone. It isn't influenced by another player, his ball, his equipment. The position of every shot he plays is determined by himself, whether teed, dropped or played there. It is this which sets it apart from all other ball games and in many ways makes it the most demanding. The true challenge of the game is the contest between the player and the golf course, or even between the player's several personalities. There is no one but yourself to blame or praise for the score on the card at the end of the day. You may temporarily avoid self-blame in foursomes or match play by offloading responsibility for the result on a partner or opponent, but ultimately the game permits no excuses. You may offer a plausible excuse to others – lack of practice, a minor injury or illness, bad luck or the excuse of retirement from major competition. But to yourself there can be no excuse at all. This creates certain mental pressures in the struggle to cope with failure. It requires the aspiring golfer to develop just the right blend of dedication and desire for perfection, with a philosophical acceptance of blame and imperfections.

The game of imperfections

Golf is a game in which imperfection is inevitable. It is not a game where even the top professional can play any round without being dissatisfied over many shots. The top professional will perhaps play only four or five shots in each round which truly satisfy his perfectionist standards. The art of playing good golf is in many ways one of improving the worst shots so that they become relatively imperceptible to the spectator. The top-class professional golfer may hit what to him is an extremely poor drive, the error in which is hardly noticeable. He probably allows for a certain degree of error in setting up for each shot, and his bad drive may only result in his being on the wrong side of the

Ken Brown, one of the game's finest putters, missing a tiddler. The game depends so much on being able to accept that mistakes are inevitable and to cope with potential frustration

fairway and therefore facing a more difficult second shot. His best shots are probably developed as a very young player and yet his worst shots improve continually throughout his whole golfing career.

It is therefore necessary for the golfer to learn to live with imperfection and not to allow one error to lead to others by a destructive mental attitude. Some players, of course, react far better to imperfection than others do. Some can remain totally complacent about their shortcomings, though if too complacent and lacking in a desire for perfection are unlikely to reach any great heights at the game. Others are likely to be so frustrated by errors and their own inability that the game may be almost unbearable to play.

On the other hand, many players are relatively unrealistic about their own ability at the game. In many cases they do not fully evaluate their own performance and often are totally oblivious of their weaknesses. In order to improve to any great degree, it is necessary to spend time evaluating your own golf but without falling into the trap of becoming over-critical and therefore destructive. The player who wants to improve needs to remain relatively detached about his own golf when he is actually playing the game, not being self-critical, but rather reflecting on his performance in a thorough and sensible manner after the game has finished.

In many instances players are unaware of the errors which are typically costly in their own game. They may, for example, think that their scores are ruined by poor putting, when in reality they underclub and so continually leave themselves in a three-putt area, or simply hit too many inaccurate iron shots which put pressure on putting. In other cases players do not realize that they hit only nine or ten fairways from the tee and instead of appreciating that the fault lies with their driving may again prefer to blame poor putting or simply bad luck. It is therefore necessary to take a long hard look at the game and yet at the same time retain a sufficiently high morale to enable the approach to golf to remain positive.

As well as learning to improve the worst shots and to develop a higher overall standard at the game, the player needs to master his own attitude to errors in a systematic way. This may mean forcibly casting aside thoughts of any shots that have gone before to the exclusion of all past memories, or it may be a question of adopting an attitude that the game is far less important than he usually imagines. The round that caused terrible anxiety last Saturday is likely to be totally forgotten this weekend. The anguish that was suffered then is now probably totally forgotten and was in reality out of all proportion to the importance of the event. It is, after all, only a game to the majority of people, and life goes on in exactly the same way despite losing a game or dribbling a drive into a ditch! Only the loss of a major championship usually has any real bearing on life a few days or weeks hence.

The judgement of self

The good golfer sets himself high standards of performance. He is unlikely to be satisfied with any round, however low the score, and is almost always self-critical with every shot produced. In order to be a champion golfer, or a champion at any sport, it is essential to have some sort of perfectionist attitude. You want to do as well as you can and you want to perform at your best all the time.

The whole underlying charm of golf, however, is that one never learns to master the game to such an extent that bad or, at best, less than perfect shots never appear. It is inevitable even for a professional golfer to make bad shots occasionally. To a certain extent the game is one of probabilities. The better you become at the game, the smaller the percentage of likely bad shots or less than perfect shots with any club. That percentage of not so good shots is always present. Even for the really top-class golfer there are going to be errors in particular shots which may or may not be particularly costly, depending upon the situation in which the error arises.

Accepting errors

What is not acceptable to many people is that these errors keep occurring, however good a golfer one becomes, and may in fact seem to occur more frequently just at the time when you want to give of your best. What is essential for any golfer is not to become so angry or frustrated at any particular bad shot that the error keeps on recurring. Almost all top-class golfers go through a period when the game is so annoying that they can hardly control their anger at their own errors. Frankly, I am not sure that this is a bad thing as far as developing golf is concerned. The person who is thoroughly complacent about poor shots is unlikely to become a great player. If he doesn't care sufficiently about the errors and inadequacies in his own play, then almost certainly he won't have the motivation to improve. But what is important is that, as the technique develops, the player learns that perfect control of emotions and acceptance of errors are a part of the game which must be conquered. Golf is not like many high-speed games where a certain degree of anger can be channelled into physical activity and can in a way lift performance to a higher than normal level. Golf is a game where the arousal level for the majority of people has to be kept under control and should not be too high. Any excess anger with oneself usually keys up the body to too high an arousal level, pumping excess adrenaline, and so leading to additional errors.

Self-criticism is necessary. Without it no one ever improves at golf. The teenager who goes into a fury at his own errors is far more likely to be the one who becomes a champion than the player who adopts a thoroughly couldn't-care-less attitude. But although the perfectionist desire is vital in developing technique it can also be destructive if not channelled correctly. It is inevitable that very few shots can truly satisfy the criteria for perfection; the rest may leave the player disappointed, self-critical or downright angry. If this anger is turned inwards, the tendency is to create additional mental pressure through the frustration of trying for the unat-

tainable. The perfectionist frequently allows one bad shot to cause such inner anguish that he follows this with a string of poor shots instead of casting the initial failure aside. Thoughts of errors need to be forcibly flushed from the mental system during play; they should be accepted as an inevitable characteristic of the game, which hardly warrant consideration.

The perfectionist

The person who is a real perfectionist perhaps has the greatest internal battle to fight. In many ways the perfectionist is never really likely to enjoy his golf. He will never be able to conquer all his imperfections and unless he can accept this his career as a golfer is likely to be a miserable one. The aspiring champion undoubtedly needs a strong desire for perfection, but a perfectionist attitude must also be combined with a certain acceptance of imperfection. Many good golfers become so irritated by their own failings that the game becomes almost unbearable to play. Similarly many club golfers expect perfection every time, set up to shots as though they are going to perform each one perfectly and then become totally dispirited by every less than perfect shot. There is little doubt that being excessively self-critical during any game of golf tends to increase the pressure under which the player is performing.

Golf is a game of mistakes and failings. If the player ever got past the stage of being fallible, the game wouldn't be worth playing. It is well worth relating the story of the professional golfer who was sent to hell as a punishment for having spent his days on the golf course swearing and cursing at every bad shot. One of his friends in heaven asked him what life was like in hell. 'Well,' he said, 'I spend my whole life going from one championship golf course to another. St Andrews one day, Sunningdale the next, Pebble Beach the next, and so on.' 'And I suppose you're going to tell me,' said his chum, 'that you never manage to hit the fairway and finish up going round in a hundred.' 'Hell, no,' came the reply. 'That would be exciting. In hell you hit every drive straight down the middle and hole all your second shots. I can't stand the perfection any longer.'

When you first start to play golf, the game is one of gradually minimizing errors, but at a higher level you have to accept that a certain proportion of successes and failures is inevitable. You have to acquire a philosophical approach to the game, enabling you to accept that a percentage of shots are just not going to be up to your expectations. For the champion golfer the difference between the perfect shot and a bad shot is much smaller than for the club golfer. The really good golfer will often hit what to him is a thoroughly bad shot, and yet those watching are hardly aware of any error. He may, for example, push the ball ten or twelve feet out to the right of the flag or position the ball down the wrong side of the fairway, much to his own displeasure, and yet it is hardly a noticeable error to the spectator.

Yet even the perfectionist shelters behind an excuse throughout his golfing life. He measures his performance against par. We are trained to see par as the standard of perfection. We are trained to expect and aim for the drive, iron, two-putt barrier. We are taught that this is the aim of the game and all scoring is relative to this. But why? We are in fact giving ourselves the excuse of missing the first putt. We build in expectations of two putts. We see birdies as the exception. And yet who is to say that a player cannot achieve eighteen straight birdies? It is unthinkable. And yet the barrier is probably realistic for the future. It depends to a great extent on the mental attitude. The young aspiring golfer should, in my humble submission, see a new standard – 'super-par' – as his aim. A drive, an iron and one putt. The attitude changes; the attack is more positive, the aims higher and the results frequently better. For the average golfer and those of us indoctrinated with par, thoughts of super-par are pie in the sky. But for the would-be champion free of the thoughts of the par barrier, it is invaluable. It isn't the same as aiming at eighteen birdies, as though a birdie is something special. It is a question of seeing the ideal standard as being much higher – and eventually attainable.

Perfection and mental control

In many ways what the perfectionist has to do is to turn his attention away from perfection in the way he strikes the golf ball and to turn his desire for perfection on to his own mental control. The physical striking of the golf ball should therefore cease to become the key task for the perfectionist, so that the objective for his round becomes one of perfecting his mental strengths and abilities and appreciating the inner calmness of his game. In this way the perfectionist now has a goal that is more attainable. His approach needs to be one of perfecting the assessment of each golfing situation, perhaps producing perfection of the outward appearance of technique and also concentrating on producing a certain detachment from each shot which allows him not to become emotionally involved in the game. He needs to perfect his ability to cast aside thoughts of past and future, to isolate each shot, to judge distance systematically and to retain the correct level of relaxation and concentration, while tossing aside his own doubts and fears. In this way he can channel his desires for perfection into something where perfection is possible – self-control and uncluttered thinking.

Fear of error

It takes time to conquer 'the game of no excuses'. Most people's golf is continually clouded by a fear. They are afraid of errors – of errors that inevitably occur – simply because there are no excuses. Instead of attacking the golf ball, swinging freely and giving of his best, the golfer contemplates possible errors and is afraid they will occur. He doesn't accept that errors are supposed to occur from time to time. He tries to steer the ball into safety with poor or mediocre results, instead of loosening up, letting rip and giving himself a chance to do his best. He forgets that golf is a game of imperfections. He also forgets that it isn't a physically

Bruce Leitzke caught off guard in a moment of failure!

Golf is not a game of broken bones and black eyes. The only likely injury is a shattered ego. Learn to attack the golf course fearlessly and to realize that errors are inevitable. Much of the art of the game is to recover both physically and mentally from every mistake

dangerous game. Errors won't result in bruises or broken limbs, black eyes or fatal injury. And yet the golfer approaches the golf ball with far greater trepidation than the rugby player throwing himself into a tackle or the racing driver attacking the racetrack. He is nervous, afraid. The game may not be physically punishing; it is undoubtedly psychologically punishing.

Errors demoralize because there is no excuse, no let-out, nothing to blame. Fear of such error can only inhibit performance. The swing slows down prematurely, the clubbing isn't bold enough for fear of surrounding trees, the danger of a bunker or lake is mentally exaggerated out of all proportion. Nothing nasty can happen on the golf course. The only two real disasters are losing the ball or missing it altogether! No broken bones; just the possibility of a shattered ego. Every other golfer will accept your errors, feel a certain nagging sympathy and be thankful that each such error is not his. And yet your whole game may be geared to fear of error and a subconscious terror of having no real excuse for your own shortcomings. Don't fight bad shots. Ignore them. Learn to accept error, discard fears of failing and stop searching for the excuse that simply isn't there. Train yourself to fail – to cope with failure – and success can then follow.

Appreciate that bad shots for most golfers really don't matter or shouldn't matter. Losing a game doesn't change your world. Don't put yourself under unnecessary pressures that need not exist. Win a major championship and it may change your life; win more money than you can afford to be without and it matters. But why adopt such pressures and fear of failing in any other situation? Certainly you must learn to play under pressure when it is really there. But think rationally about what really depends on your success. If you lose, or rather don't win, a championship, you are really only in the same position you were in before you played in it. Why fear that? Search your pride and don't look to golf as the ego booster it can rarely ever be. Say to yourself at times of failure that life still goes on in the same way as before. Your house will still be standing, the grass will still need cutting and the dog exercising; your wife and children will still love you – even if you are a failure with a 5 iron. It doesn't really matter. And once it doesn't really matter to an unrealistic degree the burden of fear is lifted. Then, and only then, can you really succeed.

Conquering the game

There are two distinct aspects of the game to conquer. The first is the superficial game that your fellow competitors and spectators see. To them, your performance at the game is largely a question of your ability to manoeuvre the ball around the golf course. All they can see and evaluate is the length and straightness of your drive, the accuracy of your short game and the ultimate score that is entered on a card. This is how in part they will see you and how they will judge you as a golfer. But if your golfing mind is finely tuned, with unrelenting concentration and unflappable composure, they will in turn ignore your errors just as you do.

For yourself, there is another completely different aspect of the game; the one that is going on in your own mind. This is the real challenge and the one that can be conquered. The satisfaction you achieve with any given round of golf does not really depend on your performance at the superficial game. Many a time a player can produce a good score without being inwardly satisfied. On another occasion the player's outward performance may not be exceptional but the composure and satisfaction he derives from mastering his own mental approach is far higher. Once the player learns to master the mental aspects of the game, he learns to see the superficial side of his performance in a more carefree and detached manner. This in turn leads to a better, less-pressured use of his other golfing skills and new levels of performance.

The golfing mind can be wildly destructive or productive almost within the same moment if left to its own devices. Harness The Golfing Mind and the game takes on a whole new dimension – fresh challenges, fewer excuses and, above all, greater satisfaction in the game itself.